LEADERSHIP LESSONS

OF

THE NAVY

SEALS

BATTLE-TESTED STRATEGIES
FOR CREATING SUCCESSFUL ORGANIZATIONS
AND INSPIRING EXTRAORDINARY RESULTS

Jeff Cannon

Lt. Cmdr. Jon Cannon

McGraw-Hill

New York   Chicago   San Francisco
Lisbon   London   Madrid   Mexico City   Milan
New Delhi   San Juan   Seoul   Singapore
Sydney   Toronto

The McGraw·Hill Companies

1 2 3 4 5 6 7 8 9 0 FGR/FGR 0 9 8 7 6 5 4 (PBK)
    4 5 6 7 8 9 0 FGR/FGR 0 8 7 6 5 4 3   (HC)

ISBN: 0-07-145013-0 (PBK)
ISBN: 0-07-140864-9 (HC)

First McGraw-Hill paperback edition published in 2005.

This book is printed on recycled, acid-free paper containing a minimum of 50% recycled de-inked fiber.

LEADERSHIP LESSONS
OF
THE NAVY
SEALS

CONTENTS

PREFACE: THE QUIET PROFESSIONALS   ix

ACKNOWLEDGMENTS   xiii

INTRODUCTION 1

Chapter 1 • Setting Goals

Lesson 1	Choose a Path or Take Your Chances 11
Lesson 2	Get Specific When You Define Your Problem. 15
Lesson 3	When You Can't Get from A to B, Go to C 17
Lesson 4	Your Specific Problem Defines Your Mission 21
Lesson 5	Plan Ahead—Prepare for a New Situation
	That Has Not Yet Been Identified. 24
Lesson 6	Build Your Goal around a Problem,
	Not the Other Way Around 27
Lesson 7	Avoid Creating a Capability and Then Looking
	for a Mission to Justify It. 29
Lesson 8	Define Mission Success 31
Lesson 9	Compare the Risks of Alternative Missions 34
Lesson 10	Does the Risk of Doing Nothing Outweigh
	the Risk of Going Forward?. 35
Lesson 11	Plan Your Team around Your Mission 37
Lesson 12	When Time Is an Issue, Plan Your Mission
	Backward from Your Objective 39
Lesson 13	Find Out What the Big Dogs Want 46
Lesson 14	Prioritize Long-Term over Short-Term Goals 48
Lesson 15	Don't Wait for the No-Risk Solution 50
Lesson 16	Take It in Small Steps 52

CONTENTS

Chapter 2 • Organization—Create Structure or Fight Alone

Lesson 1	Even a Circus Has a Ringmaster	57
Lesson 2	The Key to Accountability Is Structure	59
Lesson 3	There Is No Team Unless Everyone Knows the Team Colors	63
Lesson 4	Ship Attacks or Ambushes? Choose a Structure That's Based on Your Mission	66
Lesson 5	Lines of Communications Equal Chains of Command	75
Lesson 6	Limit Access to Your Office	77
Lesson 7	Build Boundaries to Prevent Infighting and Cannibalism	80
Lesson 8	If a Meeting Is Going Nowhere, Kill It	82

Chapter 3 • Leadership—The Hardest Easy Thing

Lesson 1	Forget the Village Concept—One Person Has to Be in Charge	85
Lesson 2	State Your Mission	87
Lesson 3	Choose Your Option While the Choice Is Still Yours	89
Lesson 4	Stand Up and Take the Hit	91
Lesson 5	Make a Goddamned Decision	93
Lesson 6	Put Your Stamp on Things Right Away	98
Lesson 7	Give Them the Big Picture	99
Lesson 8	Point the Boat in the Right Direction	101
Lesson 9	Get Comfortable with Chaos	103
Lesson 10	The Vast Majority of the Time, You Know What You Should Do	106
Lesson 11	If You Think No One Else Can Replace You, You're an Egotistical S.O.B. Who's Failed	108
Lesson 12	There's No "I" in "Shut Up and Do the Work"	110
Lesson 13	Don't Become One of the Following Stereotypes	112
Lesson 14	Know Which Leadership Style to Use	116
Lesson 15	Ensure That You Possess the Three Primary Leadership Tools	117
Lesson 16	Increase Your Number of Leadership Vehicles	119

CONTENTS

Lesson 17   Assign an Honest Broker to Bring You Back to Earth . 123

Lesson 18   Then Seek Out and Listen to the Rest of Your People. 125

Lesson 19   Be Unapologetic When You Fire Someone 126

Lesson 20   Enforce Your Chains of Command 128

Lesson 21   Don't Make Work Your Employees' Life 131

Lesson 22   There Is a Fine Line between Tradition
and Obsolescence 133

Lesson 23   Let Them Be Angry When They Have a Right to Be. . 134

Lesson 24   Tell Them When the Ship Is Sinking 136

Lesson 25   Communicating Hysteria Won't Drive Production. . . 138

Lesson 26   Communicate That You Trust Them 141

Lesson 27   Kicking Them Unnecessarily Reveals
Your Incompetence 144

Chapter 4 • The Thundering Herd

Lesson 1   Realize That Nobody's Forcing You to Be Here 149

Lesson 2   If You're New, You Have to Shut Up and Learn 153

Lesson 3   You're the One Who Can Make It Work,
and That's Often Thanks Enough 155

Lesson 4   Your Value during the Battle Has Nothing
to Do with How Close You Are to the Front. 157

Lesson 5   Help Your Boss and You Help Yourself. 159

Lesson 6   It's Okay; You're Supposed to Fight with Your Boss . . 162

Lesson 7   Cowboys and Cogs Don't Have Job Security—
Team Members Do 164

Lesson 8   You Can't Fool People about Being a Team Player . . . 166

Lesson 9   There Are Probably Good Reasons Why
Your Marching Orders Seem Screwed Up 168

Lesson 10   Build Your Team, Build Your Résumé 170

Lesson 11   It's a Small World, and It's Getting Smaller 171

Lesson 12   There Aren't Many Ways to Radically Change
a Proven System 173

Lesson 13   Own Everything You Do. 176

Lesson 14   Sweat the Small Rituals 178

Lesson 15   Bring Me the Problem Along with a Solution 181

Chapter 5 • Building a Thundering Herd

Lesson 1   Do You Really Want to Build a Quality Team?...... 184

Lesson 2   Continually Set High Standards 186

Lesson 3   Retain Your Best People or
You'll Pay through the Nose 188

Lesson 4   If You're Hiring, Make Them Come to You 191

Lesson 5   Your Own People Are Your Best Recruiters......... 194

Lesson 6   Give Real Rewards for Real Achievements.......... 196

Lesson 7   Identify Your Lead Dogs, Feed Them Well,
and Build a Pack around Them.................. 197

Lesson 8   Find Out What Makes Them Tick 200

Lesson 9   If You Can't Give Them Fresh Meat, Give Them
Reminders of What Fresh Meat Tastes Like 202

Lesson 10   Provide Those Other Things So That They Can
Focus on Their Jobs 205

Lesson 11   If Sharks Stop Swimming Forward,
They Stop Being Sharks 210

Lesson 12   Let It Be Known That You'll Get Rid of People
Who Just Shouldn't Be Part of the Team—
Even the Nice People 211

Lesson 13   Save Them If You Can, but Recognize
When You Can't............................. 214

Chapter 6 • Now Maintain Your Momentum

Lesson 1   If You Need to Scream, You Need to Practice....... 218

INDEX 223

THE QUIET PROFESSIONALS

WHO ARE THE SEALS?

Not too long ago, a group of SEALs boarded a vessel that was racing for Iranian waters. The SEALs had watched the vessel for some time. The vessel's lights had been extinguished, and it was traveling late at night at the edge of the shipping lane. It rode low in the water, and its hatches had been welded shut. Barbed wire wound around its deck, and its windows had been boarded up, except for small slits to allow the crew to navigate. Whatever was in its hull would eventually help pay for several ex-Soviet ballistic physicists, surface-to-air guidance systems, and new microbe incubation chambers.

The SEALs moved quietly along the main deck, around funnels and hoisting cranes, until they approached the pilothouse. One hatch on the pilothouse had not been welded shut, but it had been bolted on the inside. The SEALs surveyed the structure and then announced to whoever was inside that they were on board. They demanded that the hatch be opened. They were ignored.

There was an outside chance that these were innocent civilian merchants; if they had not been, the SEALs would have blown through the walls immediately. Instead, they kept their weapons pointed toward the structure while they unpacked their manual cutting devices. The crew inside could be heard chattering nervously, but they still refused to open the door. In a few moments, their protests were irrelevant. They were in restraints. Their master was being questioned. The vessel had been stopped just short of Iranian waters. Soon, its contents would be offloaded and the hull would be auctioned off in Mombasa or Dubai.

Six weeks later, on a Saturday afternoon, the second SEAL in charge of the group that had boarded the vessel sat and nursed his beer in a nondescript bar in San Diego. The platoon commander finished mowing his lawn. Later, he played soccer with his kids and cooked dinner on the barbecue for his wife. The platoon chief worked in his garage on his 1972 Vega. The petty officers studied for college degrees, practiced with their bands, worked out, or went surfing. If you saw any of them that night or the next morning, you wouldn't know who they were or what they had done.

Professionalism has been a SEAL theme since the first two SEAL teams were formed in 1962. That was when President Kennedy recognized the need for commando shock troops that could counter the growing number of insurrections, guerilla movements, and terrorist organizations in the world. Today, there are eight SEAL teams, four on each coast. There are also four special boat detachments that control the fast boats that insert and extract SEALs along coasts and waterways.

Despite their Navy lineage, SEALs are as proficient on land as they are in water and in the air, something that is frequently overlooked. They parachute and conduct ambush and sniper operations. They train as heavily in land navigation and land warfare as they do in water operations. In fact, the only real difference between taking down a beach house and taking down an inland house is that SEALs have more options for approaching the beach house because they can also use dive gear or boats. The actions at the target are the same. And taking down either type of house doesn't approach the complexities and hurdles of taking down a moving cruise ship or container vessel at sea.

SEALs train continuously and hard. The initial SEAL training , at Basic Underwater Demotion School (BUD/S), is 6 months long and routinely stresses its students to such a degree that there is an 80 percent dropout rate. Following BUD/S, students attend courses in parachuting, mini-submarine operations, sniping, communications, demolitions, field medicine, languages, and a wide range of other areas. By the time they enter a SEAL team and are selected for a SEAL platoon, they will have received their "masters" in unconventional commando warfare.

In addition, SEALs are usually well educated on their own. In Jon's last platoon, more than half the enlisted men had university degrees, and this is not unusual. Many go on to become officers themselves. All this helps enable SEAL platoons to adopt sophisticated organizational systems and conduct complicated multiphased operations. Officers, meanwhile, often have graduate degrees and have received advanced language training. If they do eventually decide to leave active duty, they generally have little trouble being accepted into top law, medical, or business schools.

Once a SEAL platoon is formed up, its members usually train together for an additional 18 months, with a heavy emphasis on small-unit tactics and mission planning. The SEAL platoon becomes their family. Decades later, retired SEALs still look back and recall their platoon days as the period of greatest bonding, loyalty, and teamwork in their lives.

SEALs have a wide range of missions, but each emphasizes technical expertise, organizational integrity, strong but customized leadership, and superb physical conditioning. Loyalty is king. Inherent in the SEAL mission is the capability to cause overwhelming devastation as well as the ability to move and withdraw clandestinely. SEALs could go into a bar and destroy the place. In the field, they could lay down a swath of fire similar to the output of a military unit many times larger if they were to contact an enemy. But in both cases, if they do so, they risk negating their mission. If they destroy anything but their target, everyone else knows and comes running. And then their mission is compromised. The perfect SEAL mission is overwhelming gunfire or a precise explosion suddenly shattering the quiet of a dark night, with no one knowing afterward who did it or how they came and left.

SEALs are the descendants of the underwater demolitions experts and Navy raiders who crept ashore to sever telephone cables and train lines in

World War II, or swam into the shallows off Normandy and Okinawa to clear out mines and antilanding craft traps. In Vietnam, they melted in and out of the jungle, riverbanks, and rice paddies, earning the name "men with green faces" from the Vietnamese. In Grenada and Panama and Bosnia and Somalia and Afghanistan, they were quietly among the first to arrive in the country. They are among the most highly decorated military units in existence despite their small numbers. Every day for the last few decades, in fact, they have been operating somewhere around the world, avoiding the media and accomplishing their missions.

Today, SEALs continue to incorporate leadership and team-building techniques that strongly emphasize effective communications, intense loyalty, quality work, strong culture, and innovation. SEAL methodology is used as the basis for executive leadership and corporate team-building programs. SEAL philosophies and values provide the foundation for continually achieving ambitious objectives.

ACKNOWLEDGMENTS

First and foremost, we would like to thank our editor, Barry Neville, and McGraw-Hill for sticking up for us through the last-minute deployments, email blackouts, computer crashes, and hard landings that came up while we were writing this book.

We would like to thank the businesspeople who inspired us and reminded us that really good people can make a big difference. These include the management and teams of DraftWorldwide, which has created an environment of teamwork and leadership. At DraftWorldwide, we'd like to thank Howard Draft, Jordan Rednor, David Florence, Laurence Boschetto, and most especially Michael Maher and the rest of the Draft-digital group. We'd also like to mention Bob Brisco, Carol Perruso, Susan Clark, Jim Kaplove, Jay McLennan, and the other mentors we've met along the way.

We would also like to thank the men and women in the U.S. military: the Navy, the Army, the Air Force, and the Marine Corps, and especially members of the Naval Special Warfare and Army Special Forces organizations. These include the Stennis Admin Club, the vampires, the officers and crew of the *USS The Sullivans*, the Polish Thunder, the Got Qut team, the MSC, the MCT, the guys we kept hearing about who froze their butts off in the north, class 155, and RS, SM, BM, JM, JW, BD, PE, TA, RR, MG, CL, KM, DJ, ET, CT, RH, JG, TD, Mr. Kuwait, and Ed.

Finally, we would like to thank the people who were back here when it counted. They are, in no particular order, Walt, Weta, Pam, Emily, Quinn, Laura, Brother Marc, Mona, Brenna, Kendall, Francis, Cara and Adam, Mike and Molly Vendura, Dee and Bernie, Mike Fryan, Jenny Spolar, and Electra and Dora and their families.

*For the thundering herd and
the people behind the spear*

INTRODUCTION

THE WAY IT IS

As you read this sentence, there are squads of Navy SEALs operating somewhere in the world. They are working hundred-hour weeks, often under intense pressure. They are probably cold and wet. They can't always call home to their families. They don't have access to 401(k) plans. They don't have reserved parking spaces or company cars. And sometimes they die.

Despite these hardships, they feel personally bound to their peers, their boss, and their mission. They are committed to their organization. They are skilled enough to be trusted with undertakings that affect national policy. They are bright, educated, and ambitious, and they could have chosen any other career path. But they didn't. Instead, they fought for their positions. They volunteered for their assignments. And they are working for a lot less than you're currently paying your employees.

How can a seven-man SEAL squad accomplish a mission that affects national policy while your seventeen-person sales team can't produce a working quarterly sales plan?

It's simple.

SEAL platoons employ proven leadership tactics and team models aimed at making effective decisions and conducting successful operations.

Business teams frequently concentrate on retaining short-term employee goodwill and building universal consensus.

The Navy SEAL organization excels at creating small, skilled, loyal teams that are specifically designed to complete ambitious projects successfully. Business teams are often ad hoc outfits whose design and membership may not be the best for reaching their goals.

SEAL teams are the result of decades of experimentation, dozens of conflicts, and continuous reinvention. Business teams are frequently organized with little actual knowledge of what worked before.

SEAL squads are filled with enthusiastic, capable team members who have been carefully screened for their job. Business teams are often filled with workers whose chief qualifications are that they have a degree, knew an HR email address, and owned an interview suit.

SEAL platoons operate with philosophies and tactics that are consistent with the long-term strength of the SEAL organization. Businesses are blighted with managers who give priority to short-term spikes in the stock price rather than consistent growth, dazzle shareholders with unreasonable expectations of profitability, and cash in employee pension funds in order to pay for second homes.

If any of this sounds familiar, you are not alone. Today, American managers face increasing demands for productivity, but they are using leadership tools and organizational processes designed for the 1990s, which is already a different business era. If they're really serious about their organization's survival, U.S. business managers need to get serious about rebuilding their corporate cultures. That means emphasizing real leadership and teamwork instead of waiting for their stock options to roll in.

RIGHT NOW, YOU ARE FLOUNDERING

You get to your office early. You spend your first hour sifting through your email, the majority of which doesn't concern you. You attend a meeting that runs late because no one takes charge. You attend another meeting that ends with everyone agreeing to schedule yet another meeting because nobody has the authority to approve anything.

Lunch is spent deciding on the restaurant at which you will wine and dine a prospective hire. After lunch, you send email to both your boss and your boss's boss, because both of them want to monitor and comment on your projects. Next, you walk a recent MBA hire through a project because, although she has the degree, she's never actually negotiated with a vendor before.

You hurry to another meeting, where you present what you know the client wants to hear rather than what you know is the best solution. After all, the client is a good friend of one of the executives who provides input for your performance review. You spend your last hour at the office budgeting for a project for which you know there's no actual money. Then you drive an hour to the "nonmandatory" (i.e., required) mixer at the amusement park, where the company prepaid for everyone's attendance.

When you finally get home, you scribble down thoughts for tomorrow's meeting on employee empowerment while you scan the Internet for other jobs that you know are probably just as frustrating as your current position, but that might pay more. You know that your peers and subordinates are also secretly surfing for other jobs, despite the recent pay raises and perks given to them.

HOW DID YOU GET INTO THIS MESS?

During the 1990s, several trends influenced the way American managers did business. First, at the beginning of the decade, several rounds of layoffs led to sweeping reductions in employee numbers. Leanness became the adopted theme of corporate America, often to such an extent that making cuts became a knee-jerk course of action. Frequently, corporate leanness led to a compromise in organizational effectiveness. Departments were slashed and gutted until they were so flat that the typical organization chart was only two levels deep. Managers were abandoned from above and swamped by input from dozens of workers just below.

Second, later in the decade, the economy resumed its expansion and the demand for quality workers grew, but the supply of quality labor didn't keep up. The lone manager, swamped by his workers, now had to compete relentlessly with other companies for his workers' services. In an effort to retain their employees, harried managers dished out better titles, more pay, and greater respect. Woe to the company that risked not granting workers immediate access to upper management, or that didn't refer to them all, fawningly, as entrepreneurs and leaders. Hell, at this point, everyone was a leader! Everyone in the company!

Somewhere along the way, either because of the excessive efforts to retain workers or because of the excessive elimination of organizational structures, managers lost their ability to lead. When they made decisions that were unpopular with the troops, they were not supported by senior management. Their lines of communication were circumvented and became ineffective as their subordinates emailed senior management directly. On top of this, the willingness of companies to lay off their employees earlier in the decade was reflected in a climate of skepticism and mistrust among those same workers.

And now? After a spate of high-profile cases of corporate corruption, that mistrust has increased further.

As a result, the business world has increasingly become a world of individuals. Corporate teams that once banded together to push forward are now like mercenary gangs. Corporations, terrified of offending anyone in their splintering groups, hesitate to rein in the warlords. And corporate culture has often become little more than a sea of managerial nomads, loyal to no one and motivated overwhelmingly by salary, convenience, and the size of the corporate gym.

This has been a disaster for managers and leaders who want to create value and get results. It's difficult to lead workers who have been abandoned by senior management. It's tough to make unpopular choices when senior management won't back you up. It's hard to stay on course when subordinates can go around you.

Enough! If you want to run a successful organization, you can't afford to work this way anymore. It's time to run your organization like a team again, and in a manner that is principally designed to produce results.

DON'T WORRY—THESE TECHNIQUES WERE TESTED . . . IN BOSNIA, AFGHANISTAN, AND SILICON ALLEY

Have you ever participated in a team-building event in which every team succeeded?

Have you ever completed a leadership workshop where nobody failed?

Have you ever sat through a class listening to someone preach solutions that would never work in the real world?

That's not where we did our homework for this book!

Two guys with several decades of experience in the trenches wrote this book. And, yes, we really mean the trenches. It was not written by two business school professors. It was not written by a famous CEO or a star consultant. We didn't make up the content in our office or den. This was written by two seasoned guys—a SEAL and an executive—who have spent many years getting knocked about while building and leading effective teams, witnessing and experiencing lots of success and failure along the way.

Our lessons were learned in the field while helping start-ups get off the ground. They were learned while planting limpet mines under ships. They were tested on employees who were cold, wet, and hungry, and vastly underpaid. They were tested in Fortune 500 corporations when the smell of fear of the ax was in the air.

How did we begin? One evening over beers, in between corporate projects and military operations, we observed that some team-building techniques worked well in several different industries and sectors. We also observed that some did not. Whether the mission was patrolling in the Andes, mapping marketing plans in New York, managing interdiction operations in the Persian Gulf, or developing innovative Internet strategies in Berlin, certain leadership and management techniques always worked.

We also realized that regardless of the situation, the problems that organizations faced rarely involved not having top-of-the-line computers or the latest cellular technology. Owning these things certainly made the job easier, but they were never the magic bullets that led to success.

The real problem usually involved people, team integrity, and leadership skills. Good people were on the wrong teams. The right people were being managed in the wrong way—because this was the only way in which leaders and managers were allowed to lead and manage. The wrong person had the right responsibility. And so forth.

To put it simply, the source of the problem was usually an organization that simply didn't understand how to hire the right people. Or to motivate them. Or to retain them. Or to manage them.

That evening, we also observed that many of the successes we had seen were not really the result of catered lunches, or corporate golf courses, or New Economy turtleneck shirts, although these things did briefly make life more enjoyable. Usually, when things worked, it was because of people. The right people were in the right jobs. People were being led and managed in the right way—because leaders and managers were allowed to lead and manage in the right way. And behind it all, there was usually an organization that understood how to make these things happen. How to promote relationships and processes that encourage teamwork. How to promote effective communication. How to back up its mid-level and junior leaders.

Over the next year, we compiled these lessons, one of us in an office in New York, the other on a SEAL task unit in various countries and conflicts around the world. The result is a collection of tools that work in the trenches—no matter where those trenches are.

THIS IS NOT A BOOK FOR COWBOYS AND WANNABES—IT'S FOR PEOPLE WHO ARE WILLING TO WORK

Be forewarned: *This book does not pay homage to godlike CEOs, legendary generals, and other corporate cult figures.* It is our view that masterful leadership and effective teams, not colorful mavericks, produce success.

Too many books about business focus on colorful and heroic figures to illustrate business lessons. This technique is used for obvious reasons— it's an enjoyable and entertaining vehicle. Examples of this are what we refer to as the *Corporate Giant and Military Legend* books. These are books about larger-than-life individuals who single-handedly run corporations and armies, and walk away with millions of dollars and scores of battlefield victories. In such books, the leadership figures often bound upward, propelled by nothing more substantial than their personal flair and force of character, leading an array of fools, sheep, devotees, and well-meaners, while spouting brilliant, obvious solutions along the way. We have yet to see this in reality. Every great leader has a great team above, around, and behind him or her.

If you haven't guessed by now, we don't think these books offer an accurate portrayal of effective leadership. And we don't think reading such accounts is a good way to increase your own skills.

Likewise, our book doesn't go into great detail about planting limpet mines, crafting explosive shape charges, and conducting hand-to-hand combat. Don't misunderstand us: There are, right now, commandos in the field who are conducting heroic operations. They use cutting-edge technology and sophisticated maneuvering and killing techniques. But we're not going to talk a lot about their techniques or ongoing operations in detail here. And this isn't just because security restrictions are in place and we don't want to go to jail. The fact is that most military tactics and most specific war-fighting techniques don't translate well to business situations.

Unfortunately, many books about business describe military operations at length, regardless of their irrelevance. Their examples of leadership are tough, bulletproof men who spit out nails. They describe soldiers bench-pressing 500 pounds as an example of operational proficiency. They recite accounts of hand-to-hand combat as examples of competitiveness.

How exciting! How engrossing!

How misleading.

WAKE UP

Don't get us wrong. We enjoy reading about combat. But when the lights come on, good business leaders stop dreaming and get down to business. Most combat techniques cannot actually be used in the marketplace. As much as you may want to, you are not going to bayonet your competitor, blow up her office, or kidnap her customers.

Similarly, few of the organizational building blocks of the military can be applied wholesale to your workforce. As much as you may want to, you're not likely to get away with forcing your employees to endure extreme cold-weather swims, extended forced marches, and other military techniques for creating intense team bonding. Nor are you likely to command the attention and dedication of your troops as thoroughly as a competent battlefield commander prior to an operation. Nor are your people likely to train as diligently as soldiers whose lives depend on their preparation.

In short, it is dangerous to use a military organization as a paradigm for business. Besides, military organizations experience failure like any other group. Military history contains several lengthy chapters on leadership vacuums, decision-making catastrophes, and complete team disintegration.

So why do we use military examples here? Because several specific cases do contain excellent crossover material, in spite of the abundance of war stories that have no bearing at all on business. So, do we teach you how to craft shape charges, how to attach the charge to a ship's hull directly below its magazine, and how to avoid the enemy patrol and get out of the area before the ship blows up? No.

The examples in this book have been chosen for their effectiveness in illustrating how to develop business teams and how to maximize their effectiveness. It's a collection of lessons from SEAL training and SEAL operations that have been tested in the business world. These are field lessons that have been used in start-ups, and tactics that have been tried in boardrooms. This book is not intended for armchair generals, military romantics, or water-cooler commandos. It was written for managers who want to improve their leadership abilities and sharpen their team's effectiveness. It was written for managers who want to infuse a large dose of mission focus, communications efficiency, and team loyalty into their organization. It was written for managers who are willing to take those lessons that fit their particular situation and use them to win.

HOW TO USE THIS BOOK

To use this book successfully, you must apply what fits. That means that after you put the book down, you actually put some of the ideas in motion. Does that sound obvious? Then do it.

In each of the following chapters, you'll find a series of solid, unsugarcoated lessons that we've experienced or witnessed during our military and business careers. A take-away for a business situation follows each lesson. Some lessons will be applicable to your present situation, and some won't be. Take what's offered. Store away what's not appropriate right now—you may need it in the future. Then apply the rest to your business, your team, and your organization, and start moving.

CHAPTER 1

SETTING GOALS

THE WAY IT IS

In a perfect world, every mission has well-defined objectives, clear-cut guidelines to operate and exact metrics to measure success. In reality, people charge forward without having all their ducks in a row. It's human nature. If it happens on the battlefield, it results in casualties and long-drawn-out campaigns. In the business world, it results in far-reaching concepts that never should have gotten off the ground, poor product launches, inaccurate budgeting, and business ventures that should never have been financed. The greatest enthusiasm in the world won't make up for a business plan that doesn't work.

Have you ever been jerked back to reality at three in the morning by the harsh realization that the business plan you put in motion the previous day wasn't going to work? On one occasion, Jon recognized the inescapable fact that he would not be able to compete with another commando unit for a potential assault mission. At that moment, the other unit was simply located closer to an airfield with available aircraft standing by. Nothing he could do would change that. What's the only way to prevent something like this happening? Map out your mission in as much detail as possible—not just how you'd like your mission to unfold, but what to do when your plan unravels. In his case, he quickly moved tactical aircraft to be based at his location.

Do you think you're spending too much time on planning? Spend some more. Do you think you're worrying too much about things that may or may not happen? Worry more. Success in the boardroom or on the battlefield does not require everything to go perfectly. It requires you to be ready when things go wrong. You have to be able to make adjustments for the guy who breaks his leg during the parachute jump, or to work around the analyst who up and quits in the middle of the week. How do you prepare for that? By planning ahead.

Set specific goals and establish identifiable paths to reach them. Duh, right? But time after time, organizations fail to do this. Every quarter, lots of smart people assume that everyone else on their team has the same game plan. It's a bad assumption. The world is littered with the bones of well-financed organizations with hard-working employees who spun their separate wheels, ran around in separate circles, jumped from project to project, and collectively had no idea of what they were doing.

What follows are lessons we've learned about setting goals along the way. Take them, use them, apply them. They might save you in the end.

LESSON 1
CHOOSE A PATH OR TAKE YOUR CHANCES

THE MISSION
In 1991, during the Gulf War, a mid-level SEAL officer pushed forward a unique plan that had the potential to significantly affect the direction of the war. According to this plan, SEALs would infiltrate behind enemy lines and begin an assault aimed at diverting Iraqi military units from the front. Such a commando strike would involve the risk of losing commandos in the assault force. After all, any enemy units encountered during the raid would outnumber the commandos. At the same time, if the operation suc-

ceeded, the main U.S. conventional force would have fewer enemy defensive units to face during the main offensive push.

During the actual operation, a small team of SEALs traveled up the enemy coastline in rubber boats and landed on the Iraqi-held beach. Once ashore, they detonated several explosive haversacks and fired their rifles inland. Despite the small size of the commando group, a large enough number of gunshots were fired and enough explosives were detonated to convince the Iraqis that they were under attack from a Marine amphibious landing. Consequently, the Iraqi military leadership shifted two divisions away from the front in order to protect its flank. In effect, the small SEAL team—a handful of commandos—caused thousands of enemy troops to move away from their defensive positions and out of the way of oncoming American forces. The advancing conventional U.S. force thus faced thousands fewer enemy troops during its drive toward Kuwait.

Why was the mission a success? Good fortune and the weather played a part, of course, as they always do. But ultimately, the mission succeeded because people had made a series of complementary, goal-oriented decisions.

Three decades earlier, someone had made the decision to create an organization that could conduct unconventional warfare. Then, a year before the mission was conducted, someone had trained a platoon in the skills needed for this type of mission. Two months before the mission, someone had made the decision that such a mission could strategically influence the war. Twenty-four hours before the SEALs landed on the beach, someone had made the decision to task that particular platoon with the mission.

Sometime during the 24 hours before the mission was launched, probably immediately after he had been tasked with it, the platoon commander confirmed that he could successfully conduct the mission. The operation succeeded because a number of people made independent but interconnected decisions to establish, reinforce, and achieve specific objectives.

In doing so, the SEAL organization repeatedly made decisions that ultimately gave the commandos an edge. This is the core of commando and unconventional operations—setting up an unfair fight where you'll have a distinct advantage over the enemy. In this case, the United States chose the target. The United States dictated the time, place, and type of assault. The United States decided what forces would be risked and what weapons and equipment would be used. At every opportunity, the SEAL organization made a decision, ahead of time, on every significant variable that would affect the commandos' mission. In doing so, the SEALs chose the most advantageous conditions possible and greatly increased their chances for success. If they hadn't done this, they would have risked getting into a fair fight.

Do you think this is the way things happen in the business world? That companies spend their time planning their operations and their moves well in advance? That they look for ways to avoid a fair fight? Think again. Venture capitalists use the phrase *hockey stick profits*. It refers to that graph that a lot of people walk in with that shows a slow growth of business and then, WHAM, exponential growth like the business end of a hockey stick. And when you talk to them, it's a sure thing. It's all indicative of one of three things: (a) the person making the presentation has discovered the next Microsoft, (b) the person hasn't grasped the realities of business, or (c) the person thinks everyone else in the room is an idiot.

The answer most often is b—the person hasn't done the homework. The unfortunate thing is, the problem's not that the hockey stickers aren't bright people. It's not that they don't know their industry. And it's not that the technology isn't available to help them. The problem is usually that they haven't spent the time to identify and understand everything that's required if the project is to succeed and every nightmare scenario that could arise.

In addition to having a good general concept of what their product can provide and which consumers they will target, entrepreneurs need to lay down concrete goals and milestones. Why do I assume that they haven't? Because if they had, their revenue and profit lines probably wouldn't look like hockey sticks. Or their list of "what-ifs" would be a mile long.

When SEAL platoons plan a mission, their flowcharts look like upside-down family trees: The mission starts out as a strong, solid trunk, and then quickly begins to split and branch out with every contingency. *You're going to parachute into enemy territory? What happens if the inbound plane comes under fire? What happens if someone breaks a foot upon landing? What happens if you come into contact with an enemy soldier while you're moving toward your target?* The splitting tree branches continue all the way to the end of the mission: *What happens if your extraction helicopter doesn't show up?*

And these are just the contingencies that the SEAL platoon can think of. Others will come up.

THE TAKE-AWAY

Here you go: *We're launching a new Web portal to sell books over the Internet. Our portal will be significantly different from the millions of other portals in existence. We'll attract visitors at the same rate that the Internet initially grew. And our sale of books and banner advertisements will grow just as fast. We'll be rich by next Thursday.*

What do you think? Do you want in?

What do *you* think?

Setting a realistic goal for your team is the first step toward reaching a goal that is meaningful. If your expectations are absurd, you won't hit your target. If they're too low, your accomplishments won't mean anything. A realistic goal not only helps you define potential hurdles, but also helps you define how your team should be organized and who should be on it. *If SEALs are going to parachute in during a mission, one of them should be a qualified jumpmaster. If there's a significant chance that they'll come in contact with the enemy while on the ground, they should include heavy gunners. If they'll meet a native guide, one of them should be a linguist.* The alternative to planning is to simply grab whatever equipment is within arm's reach, run out the door, and hope you have the right transport, people, and weapons to get to and win the firefight.

In business, the consequences are similar. Developing a team without a thorough plan pretty much means that you're not concerned about any obstacles that might arise and you're not concerned about hiring the right people. Going ahead without a plan means that you won't foresee a little competition to that online bookstore of yours from the likes of Amazon.com and BarnesandNobles.com. And it means you'll have to fire that idiot who trashed his computer by using his CD tray for a cup holder. Because each year things like this happen. People open new restaurants right in between two existing and established restaurants with the same theme, and companies overspend on top-of-the-line equipment that will be out of date before their people learn how to use them. And then they don't understand why their volume is a third of what they forecast, or why their expenses far exceed their revenues.

LESSON 2
GET SPECIFIC WHEN YOU DEFINE YOUR PROBLEM

THE MISSION

Right now, an Iranian submarine might be near the Strait of Hormuz, in a position to threaten a major commercial shipping lane. How might this problem be perceived?

Is the problem that the submarine can potentially sink merchant vessels? Is the problem that the submarine intends to sink merchant vessels? What if the problem is that the oil on board the merchant vessels might not make it to the United States? What if the actual problem is that Iran has decided to demonstrate that it can threaten U.S. interests?

How this problem is defined will influence whether the United States will respond, what the U.S. response should be, and who should make up the response team.

Suppose the problem is that the submarine intends to sink merchant vessels. Then the specific problem might be that underwater guidance systems are about to deliver several tons of explosives within killing distance of several merchant vessels. The solution might be to thwart the underwater guidance systems, or to render the explosives useless before they reach their targets.

Or suppose the problem is that the oil on board might be lost. Then the specific problem might be that the oil on board will not arrive in the United States, resulting in oil shortages. Then the solution might be to ensure additional or alternative petroleum delivery systems.

Or suppose the real problem is that another country—in this case, Iran—feels confident enough to threaten U.S. interests. Then the specific problem might be that the country feels that it is immune to U.S. reprisals. In that case, the solution might be to demonstrate that threatening the United States has severe consequences.

How the problem is defined determines whether SEALs will ever be involved. If the problem is that the submarine is about to sink friendly ships, than SEALs are a dependable option that senior leaders will consider. The appropriate SEAL team would place one of its platoons on alert and begin planning a direct action mission. Launch vessels or submarines would be coordinated to insert and extract the team.

On the other hand, if the problem amounts to possible oil shortages in the United States, it would be outside the scope of the SEAL organization to solve. SEALs couldn't ensure that domestic coal production would increase to make up the difference, or that Alaskan pipeline capacity would double. The SEAL platoon's phone wouldn't ring. The team members' beepers wouldn't go off.

THE TAKE-AWAY

When Jeff worked with the *Los Angeles Times* as it was starting up its Web site, a group was assigned to develop a destination Web site. What was it trying to do?

Well, the company wanted to make money and increase its stock price. The management wanted to develop a strong position in the interactive world. Jeff wanted to create something central to Los Angeles to grow the online business. The management had defined a broad goal, but it had never gotten into the specifics. Soon, it was heading off in six different directions. There were several different perceived problems and several separate efforts.

It took quite a few late-night meetings before everyone was on track. After that, it took them a while to figure out how they were going to do it. But the important thing was, everyone knew what they were doing. And once that was achieved, the rest was easy.

How you see the problem might not be how others see the problem. When Daimler-Benz bought Chrysler, there was a distinct difference between the German and American management teams in terms of what they perceived was wrong with the American manufacturer and what was required to turn Chrysler around. Soon after their merger, these differences came to light and turned ugly. American managers were dismissed. Accusations of German arrogance became public. What was initially hailed as a brilliant international union became, to many, a symbol of mismanagement.

Make sure you understand the perspective of those who ultimately authorize your mission. The more precise you can be in identifying the problem, the more your team can focus on the right solution.

LESSON 3
WHEN YOU CAN'T GET
FROM A TO B, GO TO C

THE MISSION

Sometimes even the best-trained commandos can't own part of an operation.

Don't count too much on owning the Riverine operation in Colombia if you're climbing frozen waterfalls in Norway. Don't be afraid to reach outside your box or above your current level, but recognize that boundaries exist. A sniper in Chile wouldn't expect to solve European strategy issues. Strategy and mission approval is handed down by politicians and senior regional commanders, and it will not always be to your liking.

When I worked in Europe, one of the problems facing the U.S. military was how to support the democratization and modernization of Eastern Europe. At the same time, we were operating in an environment in which many missions were altered or scrubbed for political reasons. After the widespread media coverage of the Special Forces carnage in Somalia, special operations were routinely suspended when they were likely to result in U.S. casualties. Missions in the former Yugoslavia were postponed when the United States feared Serbian reprisals against U.S. troops stationed in the region. The potential upside might have been the neutralization of warlords and criminals. The possible downside was that U.S. politicians risked being voted out of office if soldiers started coming back in body bags. In effect, the United States gave the mission of achieving no U.S. casualties priority over the mission of conducting operations.

Additionally, when I worked in Europe, as when I worked in the Middle East and South America, gossip circulated in the field that certain missions were not given to SEALs because of interservice rivalry—that senior officers falsely claimed that SEALs were only water commandos and thus were ineligible to assault inland targets, conveniently forgetting that SEALs are equally capable in land warfare, as indicated by their acronym (Sea, Air, Land).

Sorry. The world is an unfair place. Whether or not the situation is unfair or the gossip unwarranted, there is often little that you can do as a commando in the field to change the situation. Recognize when something like this happens. Look for ways in which you can still own the options that remain.

The fact is that each military problem is a collection of other problems. This is true both of individual missions and of grand strategies. For example, if the problem is that terrorists are inside a building behind a locked, reinforced door, then the door has to be blown off its frame. An explosive has to be built that will remove the door without harming hostages on the inside. The charge has to be brought to the door, mounted on the door, and blown from a safe distance without the terrorists seeing. An assault team has to go through the door and neutralize the terrorists. Each of these problems requires its own mission and has its own owner. A SEAL can solve each problem in this particular case.

On the other hand, if terrorists are fleeing Afghanistan, then a number of problems exist, many of which are outside the size and scope of SEAL capability. A military cordon must be drawn around Afghanistan. Pressure must be brought to bear on countries that harbor escaping terrorists. The SEAL organization can solve only a part of some of these problems—interdicting vessels and vehicles, for example, or taking down terrorist safe houses. And if a particular SEAL platoon doesn't have enough commandos to conduct the actual assault part of the mission, it can still act as a blocking force, or as a rescue force if the assault goes bad.

With regard to our situation in Europe, our unit commander recognized two facts. First, political pressure on military decisions wasn't going to go away. And second, potential operations in the former Yugoslavia, which were widely covered by CNN and where the potential for public backlash in the United States was thus enormous, represented only part of the overall problem facing the United States. Fledgling democracies existed in other parts of Europe. We consequently conducted other missions in other Eastern European countries where the United States had less cause for concern over potential casualties, so that the missions were quickly approved by the State Department.

THE TAKE-AWAY

You will at some point look on, perhaps with jealousy and bitterness, as a project that should be yours either goes to someone less qualified and less deserving or goes away completely. You will have fought for it as best you could before the decision was made, but powerful forces above your level decided otherwise. So be it.

If nothing else in the situation is of value to you, move on. For example, a SEAL Jon worked with had considered a job in the tugboat business in New York before he joined the Navy. The work was physical. He would work on the water. The pay was good. And although tug jobs were tough to get, he had a friend who knew a skipper. "Why didn't you do it?" Jon asked him. "The skipper had a son," the friend shrugged. "And my last name wasn't on the bow of the ship."

On the other hand, it's possible that even though you don't own the original problem, you can still own a significant subsidiary problem. In this case, think about taking it. Jon was with a forward-deployed platoon when they were notified that a ship had been hijacked and that the platoon was being considered as a response option. As they studied the size and location of the potential target, however, they realized that the platoon was too small a force to risk on an assault on a vessel that large. Larger forces were on hand. The only intelligent option would be to use them. That platoon would never be selected.

At the same time, they knew that a ship assault was a complicated operation. Many things could go wrong. Many corridors, hatches, and rooms had to be secured. Other vessels must be prevented from drawing near during the assault. There is no such thing as having too much support in such an operation. They knew, therefore, that they could still be selected to carry out some significant element of the operation.

Anticipate the forces of the universe ahead of time. Recognize situations where you're not going to win. Instead of fighting a doomed struggle, aim for projects that you have a chance of obtaining. You'll look like a team player. You'll be a team player. You'll be able to walk away, having contributed a significant element to the operation.

LESSON 4
YOUR SPECIFIC PROBLEM
DEFINES YOUR MISSION

THE MISSION

During the first year of military strikes in Afghanistan following September 11, ordnance known commonly as smart bombs was the weapon system of choice for U.S. air platforms during ground assault and ground support missions. Despite their relative sophistication compared to conventional iron bombs, however, smart bombs could not simply be released from an overhead plane and then be expected to find their intended targets on their own. Smart bombs had homing devices that could identify a signal emitted from a target or follow a beacon aimed at a target. Or they had internal navigation systems that could determine where the specific geographic location of a target was. No matter what system was used, however, data about signals or beacons or locations had to be fed into the bomb's navigation system. That navigation system directed the bomb's fins to turn this way or that so that the bomb glided a short distance in one direction or another and fell where it was supposed to fall. That is to say, it fell where its guidance told it to fall. That's not necessarily the same as falling on the right target.

In any case, smart bombs inevitably relied on someone to tell the bomb what to do. Someone had to give the bomb information about the signal being emitted from the target. Someone had to shine a beacon on a target for the bomb to follow. Or someone had to enter the navigational coordinates of the target into the bomb so that the bomb knew where the target was. And no matter what type of smart system was used, someone inevitably had to first identify the target on the ground so that the right information about the target was fed into the bomb.

Targets that emit signals, such as radar facilities, are relatively easy to deal with, as long as the enemy radar band is known ahead of time. In such a situation, pilots don't have to see or locate their target. They only have to wait until they detect enemy radar, which their smart bomb will also detect and home in on. Better yet, they can launch their smart weapon while they are still out of range of enemy radar, and then turn away. Then their smart weapon will simply fly on until it picks up the radar signal on its own.

Smart bombs that rely on beacons or geographic coordinates, however, require more attention. Often, planes carrying smart bombs over Afghanistan could not identify a target on the ground clearly enough to shine a beacon at it. Ground-to-air missiles and gunfire and the need for surprise kept planes at high altitudes. Poor weather or night conditions might prevent pilots from seeing the ground at all. Moreover, the planes flew over Afghanistan from distant aircraft carriers or air bases, and the target information that had been given to them when they took off was already old when they arrived overhead. The problem, therefore, was that pilots frequently did not have current target information to enter into their smart bombs before they dropped them.

Several hypothetical solutions existed. One possible solution was simply to drop more bombs or more powerful bombs in order to make up for any inaccuracy. Another was to accept target information that was several hours old or based on assumptions drawn from maps, photographs, and intelligence reports. Still another was to widen the definition of a target. Instead of a white SUV filled with men carrying AK-47s, the new target definition would be any moving vehicle that the pilot could detect. A final possible solution was to place commandos on the ground who could identify enemy forces and communicate that information to the pilots overhead.

At the same time, the United States placed great emphasis on attacking known terrorists and avoiding attacks on civilians during this campaign. U.S. strategy was built on eradicating terrorist networks in Afghanistan while simultaneously building a relationship with the rest of the Afghan population. Accordingly, any solution had to minimize the possibility of bombing innocent civilians. Moreover, the likelihood of close combat between terrorists and U.S. forces was real. At times, U.S. forces and terrorists were only a dozen feet apart. Target information had to be extremely accurate.

Additionally, because of the mobility on the ground of U.S. forces and terrorists, any solution had to provide timely information. Finally, because of the planes' limited flying time, the solution had to provide pilots with target information shortly after they arrived over Afghanistan, rather than near the end of their flying window. The only workable solution that met all of these conditions was the placement of commandos on the ground to identify targets and relay target information quickly.

A commando mission, then, was to deliver this solution. That meant getting close enough to a potential target to be able to positively identify it and either shine a beacon at it or determine its exact geographic coordinates. That meant arriving at the target vicinity before the arrival of the aircraft. It also meant being able to communicate with the pilot flying overhead. And it meant being able to hold off an enemy attack at an adequate distance so that the planes overhead could bomb the attacking terrorists without hitting the commandos.

THE TAKE-AWAY

Who's on your company doorstep late at night, and what do they want? Identifying your problem is the first step toward defining your mission. The enemy is at the gate? Your troops are outgunned? The locals are joining the other side against you? Once you recognize the specific problem that needs solving, you can identify a mission that delivers the solution. The rest falls into place.

Brand management companies worth their salt don't stop analyzing market conditions once they have identified a change in the market share of one of their products. What caused the change? Did a competitor drop its price? Did a new SKU reach store shelves? Are consumer preferences changing direction? Was a two-for-one coupon run in last Sunday's paper?

Only by nailing the exact cause of the shift can primo marketers develop an effective and cost-efficient solution. They can develop a new line extension that capitalizes on the latest consumer taste trend, for example. Or they can run a new print ad that boosts a recent product launch in a particular market. Once the solution has been identified, marketers can launch a mission to deliver that solution.

Specific problem. Specific solution. Mission. The alternative would be to spend money across the board to fix a niche problem. Two quarters of television advertising, two separate fifty-cent coupons in nationwide circulars, and an expensive new graphic design won't help that much if the issue is poor inventory management at a large retail chain.

LESSON 5

PLAN AHEAD—PREPARE FOR A NEW SITUATION THAT HAS NOT YET BEEN IDENTIFIED

THE MISSION

Following September 11, my boss in my new civilian job asked if there was any chance that I would be called back into the Navy. I said, "Not a chance." I considered myself too old and with too many miles. A couple of weeks later, I received a phone call, walked into my boss's office, and said, "Tomorrow's my last day of work. I might not be back for a year."

I drove to San Diego, planning to run training or logistics from a stateside base for the next 6 months. The next day, I was told I would soon be moving forward to a cold-weather climate. A few days later, everything changed and I was flown out to the aircraft carrier *USS Stennis* for emergency transit to the Middle East.

Upon arriving at the Gulf of Oman, I went ashore for a brief site survey. "I'll be back in 3 days," I told the carrier battle group commander. Another commando met me on shore and told me that I would not be returning to the ship but would instead be taking command of a small forward-based unit. A 4-month mission followed, followed suddenly by a 3-month mission somewhere else far away.

The SEAL organization cannot predict what specific battles will be fought in the future, but it does prepare so that SEALs will continue to have the edge no matter what those battles are. To do so, the SEAL organization goes beyond training its corpsmen to treat future gunshot wounds and training its divers to sink terrorist ships that haven't yet been identified. It continually positions itself so that it can quickly react to future situations. To accomplish this, the SEAL organization embraces several principles of change that are likely to define the future battlefield. They include:

• *The anticipation of continued chaos.* The SEAL organization assumes that the geopolitical trends of the last few decades will continue, resulting in fewer defined wars and more shadowy conflicts. Instead of going up against major powers on the battlefield, SEALs will be more likely to confront asymmetric enemies who hide in the bushes, dark city alleys, and upscale suburban neighborhoods. Unable to fight head on against the United States, such enemies will increasingly take advantage of mobile phones for communications, credit cards and money machines for finance, and dorm rooms and the homes of friends for safe havens. Accordingly, the SEAL organization continues to emphasize indirect, unconventional, and clandestine warfare.

• *The anticipation of continued technological advancement.* Technological advancement will continue to change the definition of the battlefield. Enemies will continue to obtain cutting-edge-communications, logistics, and intelligence capabilities, as well as new and increasingly lethal weapons, including weapons of mass destruction. They will acquire techniques for corrupting information and computer networks. They will become more proficient at sabotaging commercial production and causing environmental disasters. As a result, the SEAL organization maintains advanced technological capabilities at the platoon level, in terms of both equipment and training. Furthermore, the SEAL organization maintains an aggressive equipment and tactics development process that continually updates standard operating procedures, produces major new SEAL platforms, and extends training into new and diverse areas.

- *The anticipation that something totally unforeseen will occur.* Something unpredicted is going to happen. As a result, command structures continue to be mobile, flexible, and versatile. Individual SEALs continue to be masters of niche specialties as well as jacks-of-all-trades. The SEAL organization promotes a culture that emphasizes the need to aggressively search for and test new solutions, and to adapt to and overcome new environments.

The result of these principles is that SEALs can quickly adjust from desert warfare to jungle warfare, from urban environments to maritime environments, and from 35-man task units to 2-man sniper elements.

THE TAKE-AWAY

Get ready. Something is going to be significantly different next year. Consumers are going to wake up and decide that your characteristic red product color is awful. Your assistant is going to quit and take your client Rolodex with him. The client who provides 40 percent of your cash flow is going to go under. An earthquake is going to hit your office.

Companies with legs prepare for the future in different ways, but they share two major characteristics: They forecast future problems, and they position themselves as best they can to be able to produce future solutions. Microsoft maintains an enormous war chest to acquire new technology and potential competitors. Sony maintains extensive research facilities to remain in front of what consumers value. Neither company knows with certainty what new company, technology, or social trend is coming down the road. But both stock large reserves to quickly deal with whatever situation arrives.

LESSON 6
BUILD YOUR GOAL AROUND A PROBLEM, NOT THE OTHER WAY AROUND

THE MISSION

I once repeatedly proposed to a battle group commander that we conduct a submarine-launched SEAL operation somewhere in the Middle East. At the time, we had deployed a SEAL platoon nearby that was capable of launching from a submarine. It killed me to see them not being utilized. They spent their time target shooting and planning, but I wanted to get them into action.

As I saw it, they would huddle in the small steel capsule, which would slowly fill with water. Then the outer hatch would open with a faint metal bang, and they would lock out of the dark submarine. It would be night out, but the biofluorescence would give off a faint greenish hue as they swam to the surface. They would make it to the coast in rubber boats, lying low to prevent being picked up by surface radar. The surf wouldn't be bad at this time of year. Then they would creep onshore and into the hinterland, and conduct a reconnaissance of a village suspected of harboring bad guys. It seemed like a pretty straightforward mission. Nothing too much to ask for.

"To accomplish what?" the admiral asked.

"To conduct a submarine operation in the Middle East," I explained.

That was the wrong answer.

No specific requirement for the mission existed other than the platoon's restlessness. The mission would be launched in the hope that someone might be able to find a use for the information the team would bring back, not because the requirement was already there. "We need local information," I persisted. "In case a real mission comes up in the future."

The admiral shook his head. The meeting was over.

THE TAKE-AWAY

When you create a mission before you identify a problem, you're in trouble. You're going to have to justify your mission. And if you don't have a real problem that can justify it, you're going to have to make up a problem. And that gets messy fast.

A SEAL platoon should not conduct an underwater reconnaissance of an area approaching an enemy beach landing without a reason. After all, antipersonnel mines, sea snakes, and armed patrol boats are nothing to sneeze at. Should a problem be invented to justify sending in a SEAL platoon? How about if they invent an impending Marine amphibious beach assault? That would require sending in SEALs first to clear underwater obstacles to the landing craft.

So, should the Marines conduct an amphibious landing in order to give the SEALs a reason to conduct the reconnaissance? No. Marines should storm a particular beach only when there is a real need for Marines to be on that beach. If you send SEALs or Marines up against real enemies but on a make-believe mission, because someone needs an ego boost, the next morning you're going to have a lot of angry grunts and frogs at your doorstep. If you get someone killed for no good reason, you'd better get out of town fast.

That's simple logic. But you'd be surprised how many meetings, task forces, and projects are created by companies that haven't defined their problems first. Projects are occasionally created so that résumés can be expanded. Teams are occasionally created so that people can be designated as team leaders.

It's often tempting to invent a mission simply in order to have a mission. This is especially true when a team is looking for a way to join an exciting or lucrative project. Commandos are guilty of this just like everyone else. Commandos want to keep busy. Commandos want to take part in the war.

However, billion-dollar submarines and several commandos' lives shouldn't be risked simply because someone needs a notch in his belt. Billion-dollar submarines and commandos' lives are risked only to accomplish objectives that are worth the possible loss of billion-dollar submarines and commandos' lives.

It should be no different in your world.

LESSON 7
AVOID CREATING A CAPABILITY AND THEN LOOKING FOR A MISSION TO JUSTIFY IT

THE MISSION

A few years ago, Congress handed the Navy a new class of coastal patrol boats that were built, in part, in order to create jobs in a certain congressional district. They were 170 feet long, which was considerably larger and more comfortable than the small commando boats that SEALs were used to. They carried a crew of 28 sailors—non-SEALs—providing a tremendous opportunity for a rising lieutenant specializing in surface warfare to command a ship. They had a range of 2000 miles and a speed of 35 knots. That was enough range to get them down to Central America, and there was a lot going on in Central America at the time.

Most people in the SEAL community didn't want them.

Although they were large by commando standards and carried a large crew, the patrol boats could each carry only one eight-man SEAL squad and a few rubber boats. That limited the type of SEAL operations that could be conducted from them. They could stay at sea for only 10 days before refueling. They were expensive by commando standards, costing $9 million apiece, and there were 13 of them. The same amount of money would have provided several smaller boats with proven track records, crates of new weapons and communications gear, and several years of training funds. Meanwhile, since they had few defenses and little clandestine ability, the coastal patrol boats were a poor choice for slipping up to enemy coastlines and clandestinely inserting SEALs.

Most significantly, their mission was unclear. They could act as transports to get a handful of SEALs down south of the border, but there were less expensive ways of doing that. The SEAL community spent years exploring and inventing ways to use them. Finally, many of the coastal patrol boats were transferred to the Coast Guard for drug interdiction operations.

Regardless of any benefits these boats may eventually produce for the Coast Guard, their original lack of a clear mission hurt the SEAL organization. Time and money were wasted on them. They diverted attention from other SEAL programs that had immediate war-fighting missions.

THE TAKE-AWAY

Avoid creating a capability and then having to search for a mission to justify it. Unless there is strong evidence that demand for a currently unavailable product will soon exist, you're rolling the dice. If that new asset goes unused, someone from above is going to notice a lot of wasted resources sitting around, and that means cuts or layoffs. And that means fewer future operations.

This is not a condemnation of pure science projects or exploratory engineering. On the contrary, some of your future success may depend on your access to currently undiscovered tools. But there's a big difference between exploring new techniques and tools that may significantly improve the way you do business and paying a lot of money for a bigger boat just because, well, it's bigger.

Remember, part of your success depends on your efficiency. Use the right personnel and equipment. Streamline your organization so that you use only what you need to, and where there is hard evidence to support the fact that you need it. If your resources are spent in places other than these, they aren't necessarily being spent pursuing success. In fact, they're sapping other areas that are needed for success. Directly or indirectly, you're hurting your organization.

LESSON 8
DEFINE MISSION SUCCESS

THE MISSION

When Special Forces commandos attempted to rescue U.S prisoners from the infamous "Hanoi Hilton" prison during the Vietnam War, the operation was conducted almost without a flaw. The commandos trained in great secrecy for weeks in advance. During the raid itself, the commando team quickly assaulted and took control of the prison. U.S. forces were extracted before enemy forces could respond, and were safely returned to a U.S. base. Smart on-scene commanders quickly directed the team around the few inevitable missteps that arose.

The only major flaw related to the mission was in intelligence, and even this was almost unavoidable. Shortly before the raid, a remote-controlled drone turned while collecting intelligence. During the turn, the drone banked slightly, causing the drone's cameras to briefly point toward the sky. As a result, although the rescue operation was conducted flawlessly, there were no prisoners to free from the Hanoi Hilton on that particular day. By banking during these brief seconds, the drone had failed to capture imagery indicating that the Hanoi Hilton's prisoners had been moved.

Was the mission successful? It depends on how success was defined. If the mission was to successfully assault and break into the Hanoi Hilton, then the mission was successful. If the mission was to boost morale among U.S. troops, including those being held in other prisons, then the mission was successful. And if the mission was to provide proof that the United States was willing to conduct such operations in order to win the war and was capable of doing so, the mission was successful. But if the mission was to free the prisoners who had been in the Hanoi Hilton, then the mission failed.

What is the definition of success for your mission? Is it defined by the immediate outcome, as in the removal of an enemy scout by a successful sniper shot? Or is it defined by the outcome of the larger battle, which succeeded because the SEAL sniper didn't shoot the enemy scout prematurely?

Is mission success defined solely by operational success? Or is it also defined by events that are seemingly not connected to the immediate operation? Scott O'Grady was shot down over Bosnia, but the U.S. public considered the mission a success because he managed to evade capture for several days until he was rescued. SEALs protecting U.S. embassy compounds in equatorial Africa succeeded, not because many rebels were killed, but because SEALs refrained from shooting rebels during tense situations when rebels advanced toward the embassy. If they had not refrained from shooting, the situation would have deteriorated further and would have received undesired media attention.

However you define mission success, define it specifically. Instead of stating that a commando team will pass battlefield intelligence, state that it will pass real-time imagery of SAM-6 positions to F-18s from the carrier *John C. Stennis* before 1800 on 23 February. Instead of simply stating that U.S. casualties will be kept to a minimum, define "minimum." Does it mean no casualties? Does it mean one non-life-threatening casualty? Does it mean no casualties that prevent the successful completion of the primary mission?

THE TAKE-AWAY

When is a company successful? When the stock price is up? Or when all the employees are happy?

During a cyclical merchandising event a few years ago, the wholesale price of a brand-name household product was reduced significantly, cutting into the company's profits on each product sold. At the same time, retailers passed much of the price cut on to consumers, which resulted in greater volumes of the product being sold.

Overall, the increase in volume did not make up for the decrease in profit margins, and the program resulted in less corporate income. At the same time, the increase in volume translated into a larger portion of all household products sold. And this resulted in the company's major competitor selling a smaller portion of all household products sold, even though the competitor enjoyed larger profit margins on each product.

Was the program a success?

In this case, yes, because the company conducting the program had previously defined market share as the benchmark for success in this program. If the standard for success had not been defined clearly, then others would have judged the program on the basis of their own group's perspective. The sales force might have judged the program on the basis of the increase in volume shipped to retailers. The finance department might have judged the program on the basis of profits.

You need to do two things to clarify success: (1) Establish what the objective is before the mission, and then, (2) after the mission, determine whether the operation was successful based on that objective. Everything else is window dressing. *But boss, we won all those business awards. We were voted one of the best 100 places to work.* That's nice, Fred, but we're going out of business.

Every operation can be either a success or a failure, depending on how you define success. Losing sports teams can be deemed successful if they fill the stadium every weekend. Inferior products can be considered successes if their sales teams persuade retailers to dump the competition. Establish how you will determine whether goals are being met beforehand, or else you risk being handed imaginative new definitions of success by employees who want to shine.

Jon was once in a war, operating on a foreign patrol boat. One night, the patrol boat's crew fired an expensive missile at what was probably a floating, deserted hulk. The boat shook and there was a flash of light on the horizon followed by a distant but loud clap. The crew of the patrol boat danced with delight and patted themselves on the back. Obviously, to them, successfully firing the missile was, in itself, the definition of success.

LESSON 9
COMPARE THE RISKS OF ALTERNATIVE MISSIONS

THE MISSION

This is where you decide what is the least risky way to accomplish the mission. A nighttime parachute insertion through triple jungle canopy might not definitively destroy your chances of success, but it will probably hurt them. On the other hand, a broken outboard engine will probably not affect a rubber boat insertion, depending on how fast the engine can be replaced with a spare.

This is not a science for determining how risky a mission is. It's a tool for comparing risks between missions. Unless you can accurately quantify risk, you're still working with hunches on how things should be, gut feelings about the enemy, and your jagged sense of experience. There are no statistics available that can determine the likelihood that a wounded sniper will be able to make a clean shot, a parachutist will safely crash through jungle canopy, or a boat crew will be able to quickly swap out a broken engine.

Instead, this is where you get to decide how big your pants are. SEAL mission commanders make the call on which kind of underwater reconnaissance to do after listening to the sea daddies who have been around the world several times. After searching through their own memories for something that resembles their current situation. And after reaching deep down inside. Then the call is often the best of two options. And in the end, no matter how it's done, divers still have to go in at night and get wet.

For each risk, assess both the chance that the risk will occur and the consequences of the risk's occurring. An improperly loaded bullet is not likely to happen on a reconnaissance mission, and its impact would probably not be mission-defeating. That's a low-risk event with limited consequences. On the other hand, a daylight helicopter insertion over a fortified border is likely to result in antiaircraft missiles being fired, which would probably end everyone's sunny day. That's a high-risk event with cata-strophic consequences. Everything else is in between.

THE TAKE-AWAY

Place your bets where they count. The potential reward from developing software that will serve 50 million consumers is a lot greater than that from developing software that will serve 5 million. What if the potentially more popular software takes twice as long to develop? You're still better off backing that venture, everything else being equal. What if software writers for the more popular program cost twice as much to employ? What if bugs in the more popular system will lead to $2 million in returns? Now the risks are growing greater. What if a competitor began develop-ing comparable software 3 weeks before you?

The math adds up easily. The other things—the unquantifiables—are more difficult. Here's a question: How much less would your salary be and how much less authority would you have if you didn't have to make such decisions?

LESSON 10
DOES THE RISK OF DOING NOTHING OUTWEIGH THE RISK OF GOING FORWARD?

THE MISSION

The task here is to decide whether all the equations you've done so far jus-tify risking the happiness, health, and lives of those who depend on you. You're actually already risking their lives. You may just not realize it. Take shooting practice, for example. Every time you send commandos off to practice shooting, you're risking their well-being. The car can crash on the way to or from the range. There's a possibility of hearing loss because of gunfire. A possibility of cancer because of the pulverized toxins from the fired rounds. A possibility of skin cancer from the sun. A possibility of shrapnel from exploding chambers. You may simply conclude that these risks are too low to be significant, no matter how serious a jagged piece of rifle barrel can be when, on that one day in a million, it's jammed through someone's lower intestine. In the end, you are willing to accept a small amount of risk that something very serious will happen in order to practice shooting.

What would justify accepting a large amount of risk? In 1980, the United States took such a risk and failed when dozens of commandos flew in across the desert in an attempt to rescue U.S. hostages in Iran. In 1943, Germany took such a risk and succeeded when dozens of commandos flew into a secure British mountaintop prison and freed Mussolini. In 1972, Germany took such a risk and failed when security forces failed to kill terrorists before several Olympic athletes were murdered. In 1989, Peru took such a risk and succeeded when security forces killed terrorists before embassy staffers were murdered.

How do you determine whether the odds are worthwhile? By comparing the potential risks of your actions with the potential risks of not acting.

Several years ago, several SEALs and Special Forces commandos were inserted into the upper Amazon to monitor a border war between Ecuador and Peru. Several risks were inherent in the mission. Resupply missions flown by Army helicopters were dangerous, given the high altitude, poor weather, and small landing pads that were perched on the sides of mountains. Uncharted and forgotten land mines were hidden in the mud and along dirt trails. Battalions from both countries were filled with 16-year-olds with M-16 assault rifles who were not likely to distinguish between our camouflage and that of their enemies.

On the other hand, if the commando unit was not sent into the jungle, there was little hope that the outside world could verify what was happening in the conflict. Without verification of what was happening in the conflict, other countries could not broker a cease-fire. Without a cease-fire, there was little chance of a peace settlement. Both Ecuador and Peru would continue building up their militaries. Chile and Bolivia, alarmed at Peru's military buildup, would increase their own military postures. Argentina, alarmed at Chile's movements, would strengthen its forces as well. Then so would Brazil. A regional arms race would ensue, at the expense of regional trade agreements and regional democratization. There were no alternative missions that would be as effective but have less risk.

THE TAKE-AWAY

There is a cost to not taking chances.

Jeff once worked with a company that badly needed more content for a Web site it was developing. Its current visitors were growing fickle. The time between visits was growing longer. The company narrowed down the choice to a provider of material that would not only retain the visitors, but also attract new browsers.

But the expense! It was strapped for cash. If it purchased the content it needed, it might not be able to purchase new servers if its secondhand ones went out. And it would need the new servers if the new content did its job. However, no matter how well new servers worked, they would be of no use if they didn't have new content. There were risks involved in each proposition, but the potential reward was greater if the company put its money on content rather than reserving it for new servers.

LESSON 11

PLAN YOUR TEAM AROUND YOUR MISSION

THE MISSION

SEALs deploy in response to potential emergencies. However, it's rare for a SEAL platoon to be put together with a single specific operation in mind. SEAL platoons are formed up to 2 years before they deploy to a forward base from which to conduct operations. This is because, in between form-ing up and forward deploying overseas, the platoon receives up to 2 years of training to master its assortment of skills. The bottom line is that the contingencies to which the platoon might have to respond—kidnappings, coups, piracy, invasions—don't usually take place with 2 years' advance warning. When you initially form up, you don't know what missions you might be conducting down the road.

With this in mind, SEAL platoons are initially constructed to meet the requirements of possible future missions, not simply ongoing operations. And the list of possible missions that a SEAL platoon may be tasked with is long: It includes everything from ambushes to building assaults to pilot rescues.

Despite the uncertainty over future missions when SEAL platoons are initially constructed, however, careful scrutiny still goes into manning those platoons. Instead of trying to decide what specific mission a SEAL platoon will have to conduct, it is assumed that a SEAL platoon will have to conduct all potential missions.

Accordingly, SEAL platoons are stuffed with a wide variety of expertise. Communicators, snipers, breechers, corpsmen, linguists, Intel specialists, mechanics, hull technicians, cooks—you name it. The list goes on and on. In fact, there are more required specialties than there are members of the platoon, so platoon members double and triple up with skills.

The team members you want, therefore, are operators who can handle several skills at once. You want versatile jacks-of-all-trades who can quickly become experts in niche specialties.

THE TAKE-AWAY

Don't rush out and hire the best people unless you know what they are going to do. There's little value in hiring snipers for guard duty, or bringing in Wall Street bond traders to handle customer service. Right now, sharp, smart MBAs are being overpaid and wasted in jobs that could be filled by teenagers. Great people do great things in the right jobs. They can also botch things up thoroughly in the wrong jobs.

Make sure you know what your people are going to be doing before you hire them. This doesn't mean you have to know the exact title and responsibility they'll have in 2 years. But you do need to know what personality traits and tool sets will be required. Then bring in only those people who have a chance of fitting into the role.

LESSON 12
WHEN TIME IS AN ISSUE, PLAN YOUR MISSION BACKWARD FROM YOUR OBJECTIVE

THE MISSION

Not too long ago, a SEAL platoon was given the task of providing information about an enemy military installation. To plan this mission, the platoon worked backward from the final objective, transmitting the target information from the field.

The first question was, when was information about the base needed? Moving backward, when did the members of the platoon have to complete their surveillance in order to transmit the information on time? Moving further back, when did they have to begin their surveillance to allow for a sufficient number of eyes on the target? Moving still further back, when did they have to reach the target site in order to set up their surveillance positions on time? When did they have to begin moving from elsewhere in the enemy country in order to reach the enemy base on time? When did they have to get into the enemy country in order to begin their movement? When did they need to depart from a friendly base in order to reach the enemy country? When did they need to reach the friendly base? When did they need to depart from where they were now in order to get there on time? When did they need to begin packing?

THE TAKE-AWAY

It's the same in business. Plan backward from where you want to be. A new product has to be on the shelf by December of next year. When does it have to arrive at the store in order for the store clerks to get it onto the shelves? When do delivery trucks need to leave the factory in order to get it to the store on time? When does the product have to be at the factory loading dock in order to get on the trucks? When does production of the product have to be completed? When does production need to begin?

It doesn't stop there. When does the decision to begin production need to be made? When must product testing be finalized in order to make this decision? When does a prototype need to be completed in order to begin testing? When must art and design work be finished in order to build a prototype? Finally, when does the decision to go forth with the project or not have to be made?

Setting the overall goal and a series of objectives allows you to build a team that is designed to meet the overall goals, while still meeting the immediate needs. Here's how it's done.

1. Define the Overall, Long-Term Goal of the Team

One goal of the SEAL organization is to continuously be able to provide SEAL forces on demand. After one bang-up ambush operation, the SEAL organization wants to be able to conduct another quality operation somewhere else, maybe a hostage rescue, and then another, maybe a warlord take-down, and then another. The overall, long-term goal of the SEAL organization is to provide elite commando forces whenever they are needed—over and over again. In fact, at any given time, somewhere around the world, consistent with this objective, a SEAL platoon is operating.

That means that the SEAL organization not only has to produce individual SEALs and platoons that are extremely capable, but also needs to maintain that high level of capability at all times. That means it also needs to continuously position SEAL forces so that they can respond rapidly.

In order to continuously achieve this goal, the SEAL organization has to maintain a pipeline so that the right people become SEALs. It has to continuously maintain these people at an exceptionally high capability level. It has to continuously maintain a leadership structure to employ its forces. And it has to continuously maintain a culture that consistently supports and reinforces its troops. Any short-term goal must be consistent with these themes.

What are your organization's long-term goals?

2. Work Backward to Define Benchmarks and Short-Term Objectives That Are Consistent with Your Long-Term Goals

What objectives have to be met in order to provide the SEAL organization with what it needs?

Short-Term Goal 1: *Provide the right people.*
Initial, basic SEAL training, otherwise known as Basic Underwater Demolition School (BUD/S), is perhaps the most arduous military training in the world, and yet the system attracts hundreds of applicants every year. Enthusiastic, physically fit, patriotic, extremely confident team players fight to get to the SEAL community, where veteran SEALs tear them to pieces. A fraction of them pass the rigors of training. Maintaining the lure so that the organization attracts certain individuals and maintaining the tough initial screening process are key short-term goals that support the long-term goal of supplying the right people.

Short-Term Goal 2: *Maintain outstanding capabilities.*
Once people are accepted into the SEAL community, they train almost continuously, both individually and in teams. After basic commando training, SEALs attend an advanced commando school, and then jump school, and dive school, and sniper school, and communications school, and dozens of other schools. Then they are placed in platoons that undergo a continuous cycle of team training. Urban warfare. Jungle warfare. Mountain warfare. Years go by. SEALs earn the equivalent of a doctorate in commando operations. Then they deploy to operate, and the training continues. Local languages. Regional tactics. Training with forces from other countries. Then back

to the United States and into another platoon. Training never ends. Maintaining this tempo is a key short-term goal that supports the long-term goal of providing the United States with a continuously high capability.

Short-Term Goal 3: *Provide effective leadership.*
The SEAL organization employs leaders with operational experience, political savvy, technical expertise, and managerial know-how. Officers—the leaders and managers in the military—go through the same training as enlisted personnel to ensure technical proficiency and team bonding. Senior enlisted personnel—the technical masters and operational foremen of the military—are given enormous influence over strategy. Both officers and senior enlisted personnel become regional experts, receive postgraduate degrees, and are loaned out to other special operations staffs, where they learn and leverage their skills.

At the same time, officers and enlisted personnel are repeatedly placed in positions where they can hone their leadership skills. This continues throughout the officer's career: at the squad level, the platoon level, the task unit level, and the SEAL team level. One SEAL officer whom Jon worked under in California and the Middle East has wartime experience in the Gulf War, Somalia, and a half-dozen other conflicts; speaks another language; and has an advanced degree in low-intensity conflict. And he's not unusual. An enlisted SEAL whom Jon knows can speak two exotic languages; has operated in Bosnia, Central Africa, and dozens of other countries; and has worked on several senior battle staffs.

Rotating leaders through different theaters exposes them to different methods, customs, and solutions. Assigning leaders to different missions increases their ability to grasp operational capabilities and limitations. Sending them back to school, again and again, increases their ability to shoot, jump, analyze, and plan. Maintaining extensive corporate and leadership expertise, as well as a deep sense of community loyalty, is a short-term goal that supports the long-term goal of employing SEALs effectively and wisely.

Short-Term Goal 4: *Maintain a strong culture.*

SEALs trust SEALs with their lives. From the first day of initial training, this theme is reinforced continuously. Trainees are organized into inseparable pairs in BUD/S. From that day on, they are taught never to leave each other on a swim, never to leave each other when securing a ship, never to leave each other in the field. With two people, one can always cover the other's back, carry the other to safety, and take watch while the other rests. A bond is created. Trust follows. Trust is the lifeblood of the SEAL community. SEALs pack each other's parachutes, monitor each other's dive equipment, cover each other when under fire, and give each other blood transfusions. You could be the fastest sprinter in the world, but if you leave your buddy behind, you're out. SEALs have never left a buddy behind in combat, not even a buddy's corpse. You're hurt yourself? No matter. Mike Thornton had several rounds in him and still slung his mate over his shoulder and fought his way back to the beach in Vietnam. Enforcing this philosophy is a short-term goal that supports the long-term goal of maintaining a warrior culture.

What short-term goals do you have in place that support your long-term goals?

3. Build Your Leadership around Your Long-Term Goals

SEAL teams are built primarily around three individuals who have several years of experience with the SEAL organization and who implicitly understand the long-term goals of the SEAL organization. They understand operational concerns. They know budget issues. They know the direction in which the world is turning. They know what can and can't be done.

Each of the following is a position that exists on every SEAL team. There is a rough business equivalent for each of them. What's important, however, is that all these responsibilities are handled within your business, whether or not the position as such officially exists.

The Commanding Officer. The commanding officer's job is to see the big picture and to move the team forward in alignment with that strategic vision. "We're moving forward quickly into more cold-water training," a commanding officer once announced to Jon's team during their weekly meeting. "The Soviet Union is our main adversary, and we're going to do everything we can to train like we'd fight." His commanding officer in Europe moved them, operationally, into Eastern Europe. His commanding officer in Panama pushed forward the concept of foreign internal defense (FID), in addition to their traditional mission of crisis response.

The Executive Officer (XO). The executive officer's job is to ensure that the organization runs in accordance with established procedures. In his next job he will be the skipper, but right now he's getting down the rules of the road. In corporate terms, he is the equivalent of chief counsel, chief financial officer, and the head of human relations, all rolled into one job. There are many ways to obtain bullets, pay your troops, maintain your base, and resolve disputes. The XO makes sure these things are all done the right way. This ensures the long-term goal of maintaining a sound organizational foundation.

The Command Master Chief. The command master chief ensures that the pack is taken care of. How is morale? What does Foxtrot platoon think of its officers? How's Betty Smith handling the triplets while her husband's deployed to Colombia? This ensures that people have a source to go to for advice and counseling. It also ensures that there's someone who is able and willing to tell the commanding officer what's really going on and how the skipper is really doing.

Which of your leaders will ensure alignment with long-term goals? Which of your leaders will ensure that your short-term operations are done in accordance with established procedures? Which of your leaders will ensure that the rest of your people aren't left behind?

Each of these three individuals plays a distinct role on a SEAL team that can't be duplicated or shared by one of the other two. The commanding officer can't play the philosopher king if he's dragged down into the reality of running the day-to-day organization. The XO can't run the day-to-day shop if his head is in the clouds being the commanding officer. The command master chief can't talk offline to the troops if they regard him as the commanding officer. Moreover, the command master chief acts as the enlistees' advocate during punitive movements by the XO. And the commanding officer needs the command master chief to tell him what's really going on.

4. Build Your Team Operators around Short-Term Goals

SEAL teams have several small-unit leaders who ensure that the team can respond immediately if it is called upon. These are the people who look out into the near future, see bad guys in the house next door, and get the wolf pack into their gear. Again, whether or not these positions officially exist in your organization, you need to ensure that all these roles are covered.

The Operations Officer. The operations officer knows what missions are being conducted in the field and what missions are coming down the pike. He ensures that platoons are out of the starting blocks fast, and that they are in the right place at the right time. This job is a combination of civilian operations boss and brand category manager.

The Training Officer. The training officer ensures that platoons and individuals are up to speed in the warfare skills they need in order to rule the battlefield. He squeezes until snipers hit dead-on from thousands of yards back, divers rupture engine spaces without being detected, and assault teams blow through doors before the enemy can react. This is the equivalent of the executive trainer as well as the gatekeeper. You do it his way. If he says you're not ready, you're not.

The Platoon Commander. This is The Man. He's always pushing to do righteous things with his men, and his men love him for it. He's the hungriest project manager in your business.

The Intelligence Officer. The intelligence officer lets the platoon know what it's up against, both right now and throughout the operation. Water temperature? Enemy weapons? Full moon? Hostage location? This oracle provides the answers. His counterpart is the corporate analyst and market researcher.

Who on your team can get the team to meet short-term objectives? Who on your team can get things moving? Who makes sure that contingencies can be dealt with? Who is going to be the pain in the ass, always trying to stoke the fire?

LESSON 13
FIND OUT WHAT THE BIG DOGS WANT

THE MISSION

Several years ago, I proposed that we introduce or enlarge operations in several Eastern European countries. They were great places to get into. SEALs could operate, train, and live for not very much money. Unrestricted training areas dotted the landscape. Many of the commandos in these countries had fought in Afghanistan throughout the previous decade. The media were kept at bay. SEALs wanted in.

At the time, however, there was a good deal of debate within the SEAL organization over how much we should assist Eastern European countries in modernizing their militaries. On the one hand, time and money were in short supply. Bosnia was sucking up resources. Any training funds that were left over, the reasoning went, should be spent on training with our traditional commando peers: the British, the Danes, the Norwegians, and the like. After all, these were the forces we would fight alongside in a future conflict.

The opposing view was that many of the Eastern European countries, especially those that were newly independent from the Soviet Union, needed to modernize their forces at the same rate that their political systems were becoming democracies. To join NATO, these countries would have to adopt NATO military standards. Building modern commando forces would be their best defense against coups or attacks by reactionary countries. Moreover, bringing these countries' commando units up to speed might result in our having more commando allies during future operations.

The debate within the SEAL organization was interrupted when it was discovered that the U.S. secretary of state had a personal attachment to Eastern Europe and had established an entirely new fund for operations in these countries. That was the end of much of the debate. My boss gave his nod, and we began conducting training in half a dozen countries around the Baltic and Black Seas.

THE TAKE-AWAY

You spend a lot of time researching a problem. You come up with a solution based on the facts. You put together a presentation and do your dog and pony show. It bombs. Why? Because you didn't find out what the people in charge wanted. If you had it to do over again, you would have addressed their concerns, hung onto their coattails, or gone in ready to battle their preconceptions.

Do you really think you're going to get 100 percent of your solution done? You'll be lucky if 80 percent of what you propose is done. Why? Because there are other agendas to take into account. Ask the members of your audience what they want ahead of time, not because you'll give it to them but because you'll be able to address their viewpoint. Jon had a boss who fervently opposed producing one of their products in an assortment of colors. He was all about white. Jeff wanted color but he also wanted a half dozen other things. Jeff stopped even bringing up color and gave it to him. He concentrated on the other items that were more important.

Your job isn't to get everything your way. Your job is to recommend the right action, keep the project moving in the right direction, and come away with enough to keep it in line with the overall organization's direction.

This is not to say that you shouldn't oppose strategies and operations that you feel are wrong. Part of your job as leader is telling the emperor that he has no clothes. But after you tell that to the emperor, if he still wants to go naked, your marching orders are set. In any case, go in knowing what he prefers, ahead of time.

LESSON 14
PRIORITIZE LONG-TERM
OVER SHORT-TERM GOALS

THE MISSION

Suppose that, right now, there are a dozen terrorists in a particular region of the world. They don't think we know where they are, but we do. If they knew that we knew, they would all pull up stakes and move somewhere else. And then we would have to spend months, maybe years, hunting them down again.

If the long-term goal is to eliminate all 12 of the bad guys, then the key to that goal is eliminating all of them at the same time. Because if you take out just one, the others will flee. The solution is to create or wait for an opportunity to remove all 12 bad guys simultaneously.

Under this hypothetical scenario, it would be tempting to take out the first terrorist when the opportunity presents itself. Your team has no doubt been waiting around for some time with nothing to show for it.

Nothing could be worse than to sit and watch a terrorist wander around in plain sight while you content yourself with surveillance. Nevertheless, in this scenario, the short-term goal of taking out one terrorist would prevent achieving the long-term solution.

When I was a task unit commander charged with carrying out smuggling-interdiction operations, our mission was to provide long-term interception and deterrence. For several weeks, my team worked long hours, 7 days a week. They quickly grew dangerously close to burning out. I contacted the commodore in charge of theater operation and told him that we were taking a break, and then would be cutting back on our work. "Why?" he asked. "Because the guys are getting tired," I answered. "If they stay tired, they'll get hurt. And then we've lost our capability." I sacrificed the goal of increasing our short-term effectiveness in order to increase our long-range effectiveness.

THE TAKE-AWAY

Keep the long-term plans in mind. They're the foundation of your organization. At the same time, continue to reevaluate the continued relevance, appropriateness, and wisdom of your long-term goals. Is providing quality furniture design still your long-term mission? If so, don't push out a piece of junk in order to make an immediate sale with a low-end manufacturer. It will cost you in the long run. On the other hand, by continuously focusing exclusively on long-term goals, you decrease your team's ability to react to the market. Bear markets come around, and you may have to design a low-end furniture line in order to survive to reach your long-term goal. Just understand the ramifications to your long-term strategy when you do so.

Jon was once on a mini-submarine training mission to attack a vessel when the mini-submarine plowed into a coral head. The front of the mini-submarine crumpled, and Jon's foot was smashed. The pilot beside him was knocked hard against the control panel. The mini-submarine lost its steering and trim capabilities. At that point, recovering the mini-submarine and extracting it from the area took precedence over completing the mission. The short-term goal of hitting the ship was no longer a likely option. The long-term goal of maintaining an antiship capability was retained.

LESSON 15
DON'T WAIT FOR THE NO-RISK SOLUTION

THE MISSION

We were once asked to plan an assault on a hijacked vessel in which several dozen passengers were being held hostage. Assaulting the vessel would mean coming at bad guys who were hiding behind steel, while we were out in the open. It would mean finding our way around a maze of unfamiliar corridors, all probably unlit, while someone was firing at us. It would mean trying to distinguish between terrorist and hostage in between shots coming back at us.

It is not possible to plan a completely risk-free operation. There are too many unknowns. Too many variables. Too many bad guys. Too much bad weather. It can't be done—at least, not in commando operations. And politicians who demand risk-free operations are from a different planet.

In addition, while you're looking for the nonexistent risk-free program, the clock is ticking. SEALs have drop-dead times. This means that after a certain point, the operation can no longer be conducted. The mission is dead. Perhaps the full moon will have come up, putting too much light on the infiltration route. Or there is not enough time to get out before the sun comes up. Or the insertion helicopter does not have enough time to fly around the surface-to-air missile batteries. Or the hostages have been murdered.

The key, therefore, is to produce the best solution in the time you have available. Suppose you have 3 hours to plan an assault on a vessel before the vessel steams out of range. Perhaps the best solution would take 6 hours to plan. Can you come up with a second-best, workable, acceptable plan in the 3 hours you have left? (Or, rather, the 2 hours and 59 minutes that you now have left.)

There's a lot of pressure to come up with a risk-free solution. After all, this is your team. These are your guys' lives. But if you wait too long, you may miss the opportunity altogether. It's too late—the target vessel is out of range. And it's possible that a plan with less risk than the one you could have chosen simply doesn't exist.

THE TAKE-AWAY

One of the most common errors we continue to see is the overanalysis of information when time doesn't permit it. Too often someone will want to analyze every possible outcome for a project. The intentions are great, but the clock is ticking: The competition is already in the market, the ads are running and driving business, and yet this person is still there, asking for more information.

At some point, you have to turn off the research and go. Otherwise, the plan that you'll be working on will be written by the competition. Sure, it's a bit of a risk; but everything is. Sure, the competition can't iron out every wrinkle, but they know that first to market usually wins. They know that there's going to be a learning curve, and they're willing to invest in it. How many software companies wait until their programs are bug-free before entering the market? Not many. Ever wonder why there are patches, fixes, and multiple versions?

Make the pitch. Grab the contract. Then have the software writers work like mad to actually develop the product in time.

Don't wait for a sure thing. It will never come. Life is not like that. Business is not like that. The SEALs aren't like that. Not only will a sure thing never come, but if you wait for the perfect moment, chances are you'll be forced to react and your plan of action will be dictated by your competition. And there is nothing worse than that.

Many people insist on trying to analyze every component of a plan, hoping for the perfect solution. And when they've finished, they still have to take a leap of faith that their plan is the right way to go. Don't fall into this trap. If you trust yourself and your instincts, go with them. If you don't, then hire people whom you trust to make the right decisions. There's a very fine line between gathering sufficient information and trying to create a 100 percent solution. Just remember, waiting for the no-risk solution is a nice way to avoid commitment. And by not committing to a path of action, you're abdicating the lead to your competitor. And that is committing to failure.

LESSON 16
TAKE IT IN SMALL STEPS

THE MISSION

SEALs train under the philosophy "walk before you run." And then they run. And then they run faster, and faster, and faster.

Long before a SEAL platoon deploys on an operation, the commanding officer is aware of the platoon's capabilities. This is true even during the "walking" stages of training, almost 2 years before the deployment takes place, when the platoon does all its training at slow speeds in order to guarantee that it has the fundamentals down. During land warfare training, for example, things start off with an emphasis on safety. No matter how experienced the individual SEALs are, the platoon goes through introductory shooting drills. Stationary target shooting. Reloading drills. Muzzle discipline. The training cadre looks for simple mistakes during this phase. Are the shooters conscientious and disciplined? Do they adhere to basic safety precautions?

If there are no issues, the training accelerates and the platoons' members begin moving faster, or "running." Moving targets. Multiple targets. Shooting while on the move. Wounded-man drills. Again, the trainers look for mistakes and errors and judge whether the platoon is ready to move on to an even faster, more sophisticated level.

If the platoon is ready, trainers take the brakes off further. Impromptu ambushes and fire-and-maneuver. The platoon quickly but steadily accelerates toward more sophisticated shooting scenarios. Room clearing and hidden targets. Hostages mixed in with terrorists. Complicated floor plans. But at each level, certain milestones must be passed. A shooter's habit of pulling his 9-mm pistol trigger too far to the left is solved long before he is asked to take out two bad guys without hitting the grandma in the middle.

THE TAKE-AWAY

Every operation has more than one marker. There are more steps to the creation of a new toy, for example, than the simple guidance of "Make something for Christmas." The toy must be tested to ensure kids actually want it; to make sure it is safe; to make sure it can be manufactured, shipped, marketed and sold for a profit; to make sure retailers will stock it. The whole process is broken down into a series of small steps, each of which has to be achieved in order for the project to proceed. A series of benchmarks and milestones needs to be established and successfully met before Blinky gets anywhere near the kids' toy shelf.

It's just as important to know what to do if you don't hit the benchmarks. If the platoon doesn't hit its target, that platoon needs to evaluate where its weakness lies, and it is kept at that level until either it finds a way to overcome that weakness or the platoon is dissolved. This is the only way to ensure that the team doesn't jump forward and miss essential skills. Theoretically, platoon members could immediately jump forward and learn quick drawing before anything else. But would you trust them to aim in the right direction, or to pick the right target?

It's no different with a business team. Benchmarks are critical to the success or failure of a mission. You can't make a final toy product until you work the bugs out in a prototype. And you can't make a prototype until you complete your testing to demonstrate that it's a profitable idea. And before that, you need to prove your concept with the companies that are funding it.

Not only are you establishing that you're on track and on time, you're also determining where your weak points are. Benchmarks are more than just goals; they're ways to judge how successful your team is. Is the team continually having problems passing its hurdles? Will you need to bring in additional help later on? Do they need to prepare further for the next hurdle? This isn't horseshoes, and close isn't good enough. This is to determine whether you move forward.

CHAPTER 2

ORGANIZATION
Create Structure or Fight Alone

THE WAY IT IS

Tell us if the following bears any resemblance to reality. It's Tuesday morning, and you've just set a cup of fresh hot coffee on your desk. You don't see the report you need for your meeting, so you pick up the phone and call Joan. Before the phone even starts ringing, Joan appears at your desk. "I had the team stay late last night," she says. "They really came through—especially Bob." She hands you a smart binder. You review the crisp sheets of paper inside, make some brief edits in red pen, and return it to her. You know that Bob had probably given Joan a hard time about the need to stay late because of the last-minute changes you needed, but then, Bob had agreed that he would cover this project while Eric was on vacation. And this report is important, since it will show the boss that his predictions were off. As you walk toward your meeting, Joan passes you the final, edited version, which Bob has just completed for her, along with five additional copies. "You never know when you're going to need extra," she says. Then she follows you into the meeting in case you need some backup.

Wake up. . . .

It's Tuesday morning, and you've just set a cup of fresh hot coffee on your desk. The accumulation of your direct reports' in-boxes sits piled up on one side. You shuffle through the stack, as well as your own in-box. The report you need isn't there. You panic and your blood pressure starts to rise. You check your computer, but apparently nobody on the project emailed a copy to you, either. How could they not have known that you needed it? You pick up the phone and call Joan—she's usually pretty plugged in on this project. After a few minutes, Joan comes in with an old report and says she never got the final numbers from Bob. When you confront Bob, he shrugs and says he didn't know it was due today. While you try to remember whether he got a copy of that particular email, he points to Eric's office and says, "Eric should have been on it anyway, since that's his area." But Eric's on vacation and nobody else knows what the numbers should look like.

Your boss is going to be at the meeting and you know he wants to rip someone apart because he's heard that the numbers don't match what he had forecast. You start to sweat. Maybe you could blame Joan, Bob, and Eric. But as you start toward the meeting, Joan falls in with you. She's not going to let you badmouth her without being there to defend herself.

Inspired by your increasing anxiety, you conjure up some numbers that sound pretty close to what the boss is looking for. You write them into the report with pencil and make a few extra copies yourself while the others watch. You make the meeting just as the doors close. But there are five people in attendance instead of the three you expected, which means that people are going to have to share copies. It turns out that a couple of your subordinates have been invited. You curse everyone who works for you for letting you down like this.

Which of these scenarios is closer to how your organization works? Granted, neither scenario is a fair and accurate account of a day in the life of the average manager—although we have heard some horror stories. The truth is that the vast majority of organizations occupy the middle ground. The problem is that most managers accept the middle ground or worse, instead of working toward the ideal.

Everything doesn't run perfectly, but it all runs well enough, right? Sure, if you're interested in a brief, unrewarding, or undistinguished career.

But if you want to be a great leader in a great organization, the kind that makes things happen, you'll soon learn that the first thing you need to do is to develop a team that is accountable, capable, and motivated. The SEALs rely on supremely effective teams and masterful leadership to build their teams and accomplish their missions. Do the same in your own organization.

LESSON 1
EVEN A CIRCUS HAS A RINGMASTER

THE MISSION

"Tell everything to everyone all the time." I was on a team acting in support of a small political mission in Southeast Asia, and that was the message we were getting from the officer in charge of our operation. He didn't ever actually say that, of course, but it appeared to be the basic philosophy underlying his actions. This officer, a very senior officer in the blue-water Navy, treated us all equally. Maybe a little too equally. No matter what our rank was, yeoman petty officer or flight commander, he doled out assignments purely as a reaction to a particular situation, grabbing whomever was within his reach and setting them off in the most expedient direction. Everything was an emergency. When he wanted to revise or update an assignment—and he did this often—he would grab whichever of us was nearest to him and say, "Make it happen." It didn't matter whether the person he grabbed was the person who had originally handled the problem or not. There was absolutely no structure and no chain of command. We all cycled back and forth to him directly.

As we continued in this mode, many of us discovered that we were working on projects that, unbeknown to us, had already been changed or cancelled. Senior sailors angrily spent their time on projects that could have been handled by junior sailors, while junior sailors soon learned to ignore their chiefs and just deal directly with the top. Several sailors stopped working altogether, assuming that their work would soon be redirected without their being told about it.

One evening, I ran into a frustrated and tired young sailor at a lounge near where we were stationed. He was no longer concerned with wasting his time on whatever project had been randomly given to him earlier that day. "Tell everything to everyone at all times," the sailor stated when he saw me, before raising his beer in a toast.

THE TAKE-AWAY

There's more to running a team than just barking orders. It requires setting up a system that enables you to process orders efficiently so that they go to the best person for the job. It requires developing a process and sticking to it. Because if you don't have that, then all you have is a circus without a ringmaster.

Ask yourself a few questions. What's the purpose of a team? Why do you have more than one person working on a project? If your answer is something along the lines of "the more people you have, the more you can get done," you're wrong. Bringing together a carefully chosen group of people to act as a team will let you throw fewer people at a project, because you'll be maximizing the use of the people you have. This means teaching people that they'll get further by covering one another's butts, because then they can focus on accomplishing the team's goal without worrying about watching their backs or jockeying for credit. It means knowing that if you slip, someone's going to catch you. And that means having a clearly articulated system that lets everyone knows what's going on, who's accountable for what, and where each person fits in.

Without guidance, workers are little more than a mob. Yes, that mob can get stuff done, like knocking out all the windows on a random storefront. But just try to change its direction, try to get it to focus on something specific, try to get it to work toward a common end, and you'll quickly discover the shortcomings of the mob as an organizational tool. A mob doesn't do quality work. It's the antithesis of a SEAL team. It's not the way to run a project, or a division, or a company.

We've watched sales departments rip themselves apart because they were left to manage themselves. We've watched programmers create codes that don't work because nobody with the big schematic that shows how it should all fit together was directing the effort. We've all seen foreign armies fall apart in a firefight because their communications were cut off and their troops had no idea what was going on. Why? It wasn't because there weren't enough people. It was because they didn't have a coherent system within which to work.

Situations where people *don't* automatically run to the top dog for answers, where workers *don't* automatically pass the buck when they're in trouble, and where workers don't automatically look out for themselves first exist in unnatural and artificial environments. People aren't born ready to work in a given system. They require guidance to provide them with specific parameters, substantial direction, and definite goals.

Believe it or not, your organization won't run the way you want it to all by itself. Your division won't suddenly become organized merely because you'd find it more convenient. And your profits won't suddenly appear out of someone's drawer. If you want to run a circus, you'd better have a few rings for all the acts to work in. And you'd better have a ringmaster to tell them where to go.

LESSON 2
THE KEY TO ACCOUNTABILITY IS STRUCTURE

THE MISSION

A few years ago, a SEAL platoon was quickly inserted into a U.S. embassy to help protect U.S. personnel and interests. The Marines were on their way, but they wouldn't arrive until a few days later—meanwhile, the team was on its own. While it was waiting for the cavalry, the platoon found itself extremely undermanned in comparison to the mobs that seethed just outside the embassy gate. As a result, the platoon commander stretched out his platoon's structure so that it could cover every contingency, around the clock. Eight-man squads, four-man fire teams, and two-man elements worked independently at opposite ends of the compound. These units, which were conducting operations that had the potential for severe political repercussions, were often led by young petty officers. And yet, despite their youth, independence, and isolation, the members of each separate SEAL element continued to act as an integral part of the platoon and conducted their separate missions in a manner that supported the overall operation.

How did this happen?

Even though they're working in different places and at different times, each member of each SEAL element recognizes and continues to be part of an existing chain of command. Each knows that the element leader (i.e., the leading petty officer, the chief, or the platoon commander, depending on the operation) expects the SEALs below him to adhere to the organization's high standards and work toward the success of the mission. And they know that this structure also extends beyond the platoon. The entire SEAL organization expects them to do what is right. They know that they would face severe and meaningful professional, personal, and cultural consequences if they failed to perform as SEALs.

This may seem like a minor, or even a superfluous, point. After all, isn't every member of an organization aware of the system in which he or she is working? Don't all members of the organization know what the system expects of them, and what measures the system will impose if the goals of the organization aren't met? Too often, the answer to those questions is no. Just think about it—how often have you worked with a team or observed an organization in which all of the members didn't know what was expected of them, didn't understand what was going on, or didn't have a sense of personal accountability for the success or failure of the mission? Does Bob, next door, know what's going on? The fact is that SEALs operate in a system that provides them with clear definition of who they are and what they're doing because they are supported by a system that makes a point of providing this kind of direction and focus.

In direct contrast to the SEAL platoon situated in the embassy, mobs of people intermittently gathered in the streets outside the compound, approached or circled its walls, and then dispersed into the shadows. Within this ebb and flow, no one was responsible to anyone else. Individual accountability vanished under the tyranny of the mob. Periodically, someone would stir up the mob by screaming insults. Someone would shatter a store window and grab some of the merchandise inside, and others would do likewise. A rock would be thrown at the embassy, and a hail of stones would follow.

Occasionally, the mob would be worked and stoked into such an emotional fury that it was beyond individual control. At this juncture, those responsible for the initial provocations would disappear into the faceless mass of the crowd to avoid responsibility. Within this mass, anything that was consistent with the mob mentality was acceptable and without personal consequences. Who knows whose hand launched the rock that took out the shopkeeper's teeth? Who knows which group of men assaulted that woman in plain sight of everyone? To say or do anything contrary to the mob was to risk being attacked oneself.

THE TAKE-AWAY

Mobs aren't limited to the streets of the third world or outside World Trade Organization summits. They also exist in boardrooms, meetings, and focus groups, and on the Internet. And if there is no structure, a mob mentality will develop that will eat away at an organization's resources, profits, and success.

Have you ever seen this happen? Someone in a smart, professional company talks up an idea in a meeting. Others join in, either because the idea's cool or trendy or because whoever has the idea is intimidating or respected. Their testimony is seen as the endorsement of the crowd. The weight of their collective opinion continues to roll forward through meetings and email, continuously gaining strength as still others either jump on board or scurry out of the way to hide. Finally, by the time the idea is approved and becomes a plan, its author claims to have achieved "buy-in" within the company.

No one is willing to say that the emperor has no clothes. No one is about to risk salary or career path by defying the mob. The mob rules.

A mob mentality can occur even at companies that place great value on diversity of ideas and thinking outside the box. We've both worked for companies that were run by smart people who had smart analysts, technicians, and testers at their disposal. But none of that made any difference if accountability was not maintained.

In developing this book, Jeff recounted a story from early in his career. He worked for a proven product company which had become a leader in its category. When he first came on board, he wanted to know more, so he asked a coworker to show him examples of the competitor's products. She held up what appeared to be a sleeker, more contemporary model than ours. Even before you saw how well it worked, you could just tell that it was going to be *better*.

"How much does it cost?" he asked.

"Less than ours," she answered.

An uneasy silence followed.

"But we've done lots of testing," she quickly said with a smile. "Consumers are very content with our product."

"Perhaps it's just my taste," Jeff remembered thinking. But deep down inside, he remembered feeling uncomfortable about a competitive product that seemed to him to look better and that cost significantly less. But who was he to say? He was the new guy.

He soon learned that the consumer tests my coworker had spoken of, which seemingly validated consumer satisfaction, had been conducted before the release of our competitor's product. However, no one felt inclined to be the one to bring up that unfortunate fact, so they all continued to insist on the natural superiority of the company's product. The boss felt that he couldn't go against so many experts. And a few months later, the competitor had a huge chunk of change and market share that should have been theirs.

LESSON 3
THERE IS NO TEAM UNLESS
EVERYONE KNOWS THE TEAM COLORS

THE MISSION

A sniper element is a tight, cohesive team that's designed to consistently take out a target of great significance at a great distance. It's usually made up of only two people. One of them, the sniper, shoots a high-powered rifle with a scope the size of a small observatory telescope. The other, the spotter, identifies and assesses targets, evaluates shooting conditions, and monitors the target environment. The two don't need to communicate verbally with each other. And typically, neither of them is an officer. In fact, I've never heard of one member of a sniper team having to pull rank on the other.

If structure is so important, why do sniper teams operate so flawlessly when no signs of structure or hierarchy are apparent in their composition? How do they maintain a sense of teamwork when there is no officer to guide and manage them? Commando sniper teams are successful not only because both members of the team thoroughly understand what their goals are, but also because they wholeheartedly believe that accomplishing those goals is wholly dependent on their ability to work together effectively. The sniper team is successful because the organization has specifically defined its goals ("Eliminate the leader of the guerrillas and return to such-and-such coordinates") and made it clear that the accomplishment of the goal is valued above personal, "look at me" kinds of achievement. In fact, both members of the sniper team know that such personal aggrandizement can destroy their sense of teamwork and doom the mission. They understand this because the SEAL organization has shown them how they can infiltrate deep into enemy territory and make a difficult shot if they work together and how they'll be discovered or miss an easy shot if they work as two honchos. They both know that the SEAL organization has ensured that each of them has been fully trained. They each know that the SEAL organization has ensured that their partner is a true believer. They each know that although they are temporarily geographically alone, they are still part of a system in which subordinates, peers, and senior leaders exist over the next ridge, overhead in the helicopter, or back at the command center.

The clear goals and structure communicated to the sniper team are almost liberating during the sniper operation, freeing the team members to contribute wholeheartedly to the team effort without worrying about the guy next to them.

THE TAKE-AWAY

Have you ever seen a team fall apart during a presentation? You know, glares, stares, and evil looks are traded while the room falls silent. Some are preparing to defend themselves. Some are ready to pounce: Screw the company; maybe I can make myself look good.

Have you ever seen a presentation work so smoothly that the sell is a done deal before the final slide is on the screen? When the latter happens, it is almost always because this is a well-coordinated team in which all the members are working in concert toward a common goal. Petty, personal stuff has been put in their back pockets. They have willingly signed on to an organization that encourages them to act in such a way. Teams achieve excellence when each participant understands his or her role and all members apply themselves to their roles in order to support the overall mission. That, right there, is a system. And teams that don't have one don't work well. They fail.

Do you want to succeed? Make sure you have a system in place. It doesn't have to be big, but it does have to have several elements.

First, team members must recognize that they will benefit or suffer depending on whether the overall mission succeeds. *Regardless of how sophisticated my individual programming is, it has to fit superbly into the overall software plan, which must fit superbly into the marketing strategy so that our sales reps can make their numbers.* Or, as SEAL sniper element members understand, their shot doesn't just have to be on target, it has to be on target when and where it is supposed to be in order to support the bigger picture.

Second, participants should be made to understand that they are in the same boat as their teammates. It needs to be explained, or even demonstrated, that the success of each individual really is dependent on the success of the group. Once a team or organization achieves this understanding on a personal level, it will promote a culture of personal accountability. *I know that our other programmers, marketing managers, and sales reps need me to successfully deliver my piece of the project in order to do their jobs effectively, and that only if they do their jobs effectively will we reach our goals with the product launch.* The SEAL sniper knows that the spotter has passed on outstanding data because the spotter's future is also riding on this shot.

Third, all participants must understand that they have the responsibility to communicate their concerns without fear of retribution. *The new programmer just found a flaw that invalidates one of our claims.* Numerous SEAL operations have been altered or canceled after a SEAL chief told a platoon commander, "That mission concept's messed up; it won't work."

Finally, each participant must know that there is a process in place to evaluate each participant's contribution to the overall success or failure of the mission. Again, this doesn't mean encouraging personal achievement at the expense of the mission—it means making sure that each team member knows that if another member isn't doing his or her part to achieve the mission's goals, the slacker will be held accountable. During SEAL postoperation briefings, operators and their bosses walk through every movement and decision to determine what went well during the mission and what didn't.

These conditions can exist only if a structure has been put in place that, on the one hand, gives its members responsibility for achieving the mission's goals and, on the other hand, enforces accountability.

LESSON 4
SHIP ATTACKS OR AMBUSHES?
CHOOSE A STRUCTURE THAT'S
BASED ON YOUR MISSION

THE MISSION

SEALs operate effectively in both centralized and dispersed autonomous structures, depending on their objective. My platoon was once given a training mission of placing limpet mines on a target vessel that was moored in a harbor with strong, unpredictable currents. We knew that maintaining a straight course through the darkness (it was a nighttime operation, of course) while being battered by those currents would be challenging in the extreme. Moreover, the target was not going to be easy to find. It was moored to a pier, but that wasn't really a distinguishing characteristic in this busy harbor. Dozens of other ships were moored close by, and from our underwater vantage point, they would all appear similar to the target vessel. Finally, the water itself was no treat, littered as it was with pilings, lines, nets, and wreckage. Sediment and algae limited visibility to 3 or 4 feet at most. On top of all this, we had only a limited amount of time to reach the target vessel, plant the mines, and remove to a safe distance. We couldn't spend a lot of time searching the harbor until we found the right target.

To ensure that we found the right vessel and attached a mine, we split up into half a dozen independent dive pairs. Each pair had the capability and authority to individually find and sink the vessel. We planned the mission together and were inserted as a team out at sea, infiltrating together in a pair of rubber boats to get close to the harbor. Once there, we spent a few hours tied to an old fishing buoy while we waited for our window of opportunity to arrive. During this time, we adjusted our plans to take into account the ship traffic we had seen. We set our drop-dead time and our rendezvous time. Then, in individual pairs, we slipped into the water. Within seconds, we lost sight of one another. Each pair swam into the harbor by themselves, navigated past piers and around nets, and independently located the target. Or, after failing to locate the target in a certain period of time, they evaluated their situation, determined that they could no longer reach the target and make it back to the rendezvous point, and aborted their attempt. Only one dive pair had to make it to the vessel in order to sink it. If more than one team made it, great—overkill. But everyone knew when the drop-dead time was, and when they had to get out of the target area. In order to accomplish the goal of this mission—plant a limpet mine on a specific ship—I decided to adopt a flexible structure that required my team to work independently toward a common goal.

A short time after we conducted our ship attack, my platoon was given the training mission of conducting an ambush. We patrolled overland until we arrived at our ambush site, moving quickly but cautiously in an established formation that I directed from near the front. My point man was the eyes and ears for what lay ahead. My radioman, close by, provided a connection with the rest of the world, and my rear security man watched the group's back. Hand signals were continuously passed up and down the line. At times I would redirect the course or increase or decrease the spacing between platoon members to account for changes in the terrain or the likelihood of encountering the enemy.

The ambush site lay along a stretch of dirt road, in a series of low-lying, wooded hills, far from any intersection. The site was chosen to allow for direct communication within the platoon at all times. To further facilitate communication, I established our central control point behind a clump of large trees. I sent out flank and rear security teams that I remained in constant contact with. The ambush team itself was arranged parallel to the road and in such a way that everyone could see my gestures in case the roar of gunfire drowned out my shouts.

The ambush went down in a well-orchestrated manner. My left flank warned me that our target was coming down the road, and I passed this information on to the other team members. I initiated and then halted a well-coordinated spray of gunfire. I sent out search teams that retrieved intelligence and weapons. I brought in the flanks and told my point man to take us out along a route I had previously established. We patrolled out in a well-established order that I controlled from near the front. In contrast to the earlier mission, this one was carried out using a more centralized structure, where I was in control at all times and my team was expected to look to me for direction and guidance as to how we were going to accomplish the mission objective.

THE TAKE-AWAY

No single structure is ideal for all missions. It's a mistake to get caught up in the notion that a particular way of organizing your people will be the solution to all your problems. Successful leaders must be flexible, and that flexibility should extend to the way they structure their organizations. These structures must not be written in stone. They should be created to fit the mission and the tasks at hand. Without continual and intelligent modification, they will work only in the best of circumstances and fall apart when the situation changes. This means defining your structure by your hierarchy rather than by a set process of protocol.

Don't confuse the structure of individual teams you organize to accomplish specific missions with the overall system that governs your organization. A structure is the way you organize the components of your team in order to give the team the best chance of achieving the mission. It leverages and complements the hierarchy and chain of command that already exists within your organizational unit. This hierarchy should remain consistent even when the structure of the unit changes. Different teams and different circumstances require different levels of reporting and flexibility, but they all require structures in which there are well-defined areas of responsibility, chains of command, and channels of communication.

There are several basic structures. These include the following:

The Pyramid

Lines of communication and decision-making authority are pushed far down.

In a SEAL platoon, the platoon commander is in charge. Operationally, he controls two squads when in the field, one run by his assistant platoon commander, and the other run by him. Each squad contains two fire teams. Within the platoon commander's squad, the platoon commander runs one fire team, and the chief runs another. Within the other squad, the assistant runs one fire team, and the leading petty officer runs the other. Within each fire team are two two-person elements. Information is passed up and down the pyramid. Decisions are made at the element, fire team, squad, or platoon level, depending on which is most effective.

The advantage of this structure is effective and immediate decision-making authority while under fire. "Squad one, initiate fire against the south side of the compound in 5 minutes and cease fire in 7. We'll assault from the west at that time." This system works when individual operators act in accordance with standard operating procedures and the leader's decisions are limited to those that affect the entire team.

The disadvantage of this structure is the additional time that is needed to formulate alternative plans or communicate additional information that originates at the bottom. The additional time required for information to pass from the bottom to the top may prevent alternative plans and additional information from being used. For example, once the door is breached, you're going through. You have to rely on what you know right now. You've just alerted the bad guys that you're here. They know where you are. Now it's a race to see who can get their weapons on line first. You already have yours in your hands. You have to go through the door. If you wait, you lose your advantage. At this point, if someone in the back of the train suddenly has a new brilliant idea for how the operation should have been conducted, to hell with that. There's no time to pass it up—unless it's an emergency (ambush!). You have to go through the door now!

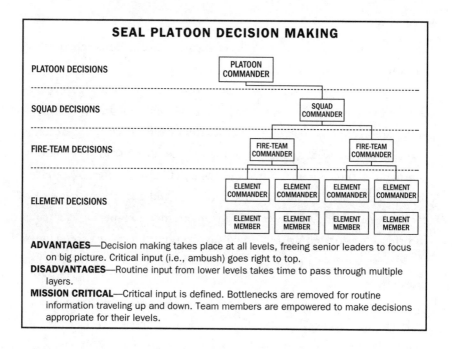

SEAL PLATOON DECISION MAKING

ADVANTAGES—Decision making takes place at all levels, freeing senior leaders to focus on big picture. Critical input (i.e., ambush) goes right to top.

DISADVANTAGES—Routine input from lower levels takes time to pass through multiple layers.

MISSION CRITICAL—Critical input is defined. Bottlenecks are removed for routine information traveling up and down. Team members are empowered to make decisions appropriate for their levels.

Flat Land

Flat land is where managers are smothered, and it's what exists in many companies today.

There is no exact SEAL equivalent of this structure, but if there were, every SEAL petty officer in a platoon would work directly for the platoon commander. The assistant platoon commander, chief, and leading petty officer would each have been fired to save money. Instead of going through these three midlevel leaders, the platoon commander would spend all his time attending to each of the 12 SEALs who remained. Monitoring each of their projects. Mentoring each of them. Counseling each of them. Training each of them.

The advantage of this structure is that information flows directly from the bottom to the top. "Lieutenant, do you have 15 minutes? And there are a whole bunch of guys behind me." There are significant savings to be had from not having to pay middle management. In the SEAL platoon, middle management refers to the assistant platoon commander, chief, and leading petty officer whom you just axed. *Congratulations, sir. The savings from axing all those middle managers translated into a nice bump in your stock options.*

The disadvantage of this structure is the amount of information that remaining managers have to absorb and the number of low-level decisions that they're forced to make, which distract them from doing things like managing. In this structure, the managers who are left are faced with the need to do not only their own job but the jobs of all the managers who were eliminated in order to achieve the flat structure.

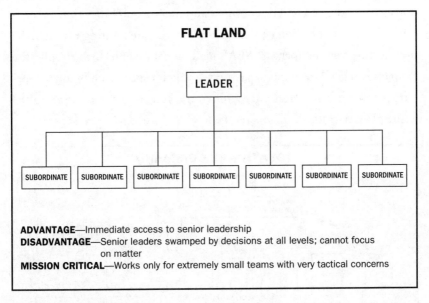

FLAT LAND

LEADER

SUBORDINATE · SUBORDINATE · SUBORDINATE · SUBORDINATE · SUBORDINATE · SUBORDINATE · SUBORDINATE

ADVANTAGE—Immediate access to senior leadership
DISADVANTAGE—Senior leaders swamped by decisions at all levels; cannot focus on matter
MISSION CRITICAL—Works only for extremely small teams with very tactical concerns

Rotating Cycles

The chain of command rotates through different people, depending on the situation.

Jon's team trained in a demolition raid during which a special boat detachment commander inserted it deep inside a thick swamp. He led the patrol to the target. Once there, Jon led the assault. Jon's leading petty officer led the demolition raid to destroy the compound. Jon led the patrol out. By the end of the day, four different people had led various phases of the operation.

The advantage of this structure is that the best person is always in charge of the job. The team can excel in every phase of an operation, not just the phases in which the boss is experienced. Jon's platoon could run sniper operations and high-altitude parachute jumps even though Jon wasn't sniper- or HALO-qualified himself.

The disadvantage of using this structure is that it requires you to have trustworthy experts to whom you as a leader feel comfortable handing power. This isn't a problem in SEAL platoons. However, continually rotating different people through leadership positions can lead to a gradual decay in the authority of the permanent leader. Those who are further down the food chain will be confused and mistrustful if they don't understand the rotation or don't trust the leaders who are rotating through. To prevent this from happening, SEAL platoon commanders, chiefs, and fire team leaders hand over temporary power only for specific tasks and for specific periods of time, and only after communicating the rotation to the entire platoon prior to the operation.

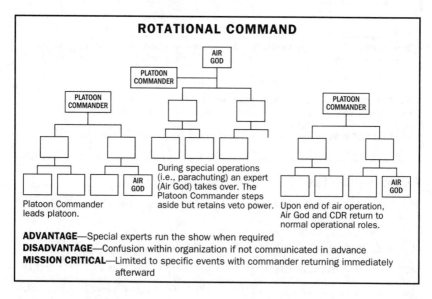

ROTATIONAL COMMAND

AIR GOD

PLATOON COMMANDER

PLATOON COMMANDER

PLATOON COMMANDER

AIR GOD

AIR GOD

Platoon Commander leads platoon.

During special operations (i.e., parachuting) an expert (Air God) takes over. The Platoon Commander steps aside but retains veto power.

Upon end of air operation, Air God and CDR return to normal operational roles.

ADVANTAGE—Special experts run the show when required
DISADVANTAGE—Confusion within organization if not communicated in advance
MISSION CRITICAL—Limited to specific events with commander returning immediately afterward

ACTION STEPS

What structure should you use? How do you combine structures to meet your needs? That depends on what your company does, what you want to achieve, and how quickly you have to achieve it. The more urgent, the more pressing, or the more problematic a project is, the more structure it requires. The more time you have and the greater the budget, the more flexibility you can allow for. However, for every bit of structure you lose, you also lose control over the project. That may translate into a loss of time and a loss in profits.

Realize, though, that adequate structure does not mean having a taskmaster oversee everything. Adequate structure means having a solid foundation, strong framework, and inherent longevity to support your organization so that there is no need for a taskmaster. Furthermore, just because a company requires a highly creative environment doesn't mean that it doesn't need structure. Both fortresses and tepees have structure.

No matter what structure or combination of structures you use, however, some things remain a good idea:

1. *Limit the number of your direct subordinates.* Even in a flat organization, don't overwhelm managers with excessive numbers of direct reports. Limit the number of direct reports to seven people, depending on the size of the project. Any more than seven and you become unable to direct them effectively. If there are more people in a given team or division, have seven report to you and have the rest of the people report to one of those seven. Repeat this down the hierarchy. And make sure each of your subordinates knows where the buck stops.

2. *Appoint one person on each project as a project leader.* This is your potential replacement so do this right. Make sure you communicate to the rest of the team who that person is and what his or her responsibilities are. Give that person power and other people to direct. Make sure the project leader understands whom he or she is accountable to.

3. *Set up teams of specialists for special projects requiring niche expertise.* Hand the leadership of the team to an expert and monitor that person closely. Such teams should be created for a limited amount of time and a limited mission.

4. *Encourage team members to rely on one another.* Encourage them to go to one another for information and to discuss issues and problems.

You don't have the time to handle many of the problems that could be resolved far away from you. They're smart people; they'll do just fine.

5. *Hold weekly or monthly status meetings to ensure that everyone is aware of what's going on.* Go around the table. Everyone gets one minute. If someone goes off on a tangent, cut the speaker off. Do that enough times, and others will begin enforcing the rule also. Everyone will come away with an up-to-date snapshot on what's going on.

6. *Ensure that the lines of communication are two-way.* While orders and strategies are developed at the higher levels and tactics are developed by those closer to the field, people all along the chain of command need to know about both of them. See that this happens by ensuring that information is assiduously pushed up to higher levels by junior members of the hierarchy and pushed down from senior executives to the people who make it happen. Find the person in the middle who's unnecessarily holding things up and bring that person into line harshly.

7. *Establish definitions for critical and noncritical information.* Educate members of your hierarchy to recognize which information needs to be passed up or disseminated throughout the organization.

8. *Ensure that everyone understands the big picture.* Everyone needs to know about issues facing the team. This means that it's okay to ask questions outside your particular box. The more your people learn about their organization, the more they can do to help.

Do these guidelines work? Yes. Why? Because the right information is allowed to pass between levels. Workers know what needs to be passed up and down—and what doesn't. Managers aren't overwhelmed. Everyone knows how they fit into the bigger picture. The less time managers need to spend micromanaging other people's jobs, the more time they can spend efficiently running their businesses.

LESSON 5
LINES OF COMMUNICATIONS
EQUAL CHAINS OF COMMAND

THE MISSION

When I was deployed in East Asia, an intelligence commander asked me if I could arrange for communication from a platoon in the field to be relayed directly back to his intelligence shop. There, various admirals and commanders from several organizations could watch and learn what was really happening on the ground.

I told him I couldn't make it happen. Why couldn't I? Not because we couldn't put our hands on the right technology. We have things that make James Bond's gadgets look like kids' toys. And it wasn't because of timing. We can get a team anywhere we want to before you even know we've launched.

The reason was simple. The last thing I wanted was for additional commanders to be added to the platoon commander's immediate chain of command. I was assured that this new audience wouldn't interfere or step in, but I didn't want to take the chance. Come on—all that brass in one room? It would be so easy for one of them to simply open up a channel and ask the platoon a question. And then that question would become a comment, or a suggestion, or guidance. Then whom would the platoon be working for? Their SEAL boss, or this new high-ranking official halfway across the world?

THE TAKE-AWAY

Many of today's businesses have cut back and trimmed down so far that they've become decentralized and unstructured, often to a far greater degree than anyone should have allowed.

Why did this happen? Some organizations are flat because of financial necessity—they've cut back the waste in order to create more efficient organizations. Some sought to replace a traditional structure with the

Internet, relying on new technology and email instead of a chain of command. After all, instant messages and Web sites are great communication tools, allowing people to communicate anytime and anywhere. And for some of these, operating with a "less is more" paradigm, less structure became not only a requirement but an organizational mantra.

Many businesses have developed a culture in which the general theme goes something like this: Remove as many levels of hierarchy as possible and replace them with constant communication between the few remaining levels. The problem with this approach is that at some point, we start to replace the structure with information, and the two are not the same thing. Less structure and more communication don't necessarily add up to success. They often add up to just the opposite—a mess.

Communication is the transfer of information. And information is valuable only if it can be processed. The fact that several U.S. intelligence agencies had information that might have implied that September 11 was about to occur but weren't able to process the mountain of data in time to act is unfortunate evidence of that maxim. It's likely that part of your job is ensuring that information is processed in the most efficient manner possible. Yet how many of us are now inundated by more email than we know what to do with? And how much of that email forces us to micromanage issues that could be better dealt with in other ways?

What is the answer? Start by encouraging communicators to control whom they communicate to. Encourage people to review their email addresses when they send out traffic. Encourage people to ask to be taken off routing lists if they're no longer relevant to a project. At large military facilities, sending out spam to everyone on the base without explicit prior permission can result in your losing Internet privileges, or worse.

Don't get us wrong: We like information. However, the ability to manage information is often more important than the information itself. You have to be able to manage the workflow. If you're swamped, you won't be able to see your way out of the woods. You won't be able to see the big picture. You'll concentrate on messages that have no bearing and miss the important news that will fall through the electronic cracks.

LESSON 6
LIMIT ACCESS TO YOUR OFFICE

THE MISSION

I value the people I work with in the Navy. Platoon chiefs and leading petty officers work hard to become effective leaders. Because of this, the other SEALs in the platoons respect them, learn from them, and believe in them.

The worst thing I could do would be to give the rest of the platoon the idea that my chief and my leading petty officer didn't matter. Or that these men were just puppets who merely passed orders from me along to the platoon. The men in my SEAL units did, in fact, respect my chief and leading petty officer. But all I would have to do to upset that respect and deference would be to leave my door open.

What I mean is this: Opening my office door to my people when there was enough time for them to have gone through the chain of command would mean that the chain of command didn't matter. And that would be a mess.

THE TAKE-AWAY

We've all seen it. Some of us have been it. It's what drives a lot of us. It's the image of the guy who pushes his way into the boardroom or the top dog's office and saves the day with a brilliant idea. It's the thing that makes movies and sells books. It's what legends are made of. It's also something that's more than likely to cause big cracks in the foundation of your structure.

Do you want to ruin your team? Give the gatecrashers unrealistic expectations and let them keep crashing. Since they don't know the playing field or understand the nuances of what's going on behind the scenes, chances are that their mad dash forward is only going to waste everyone else's time. The reason we adhere to the chain of command is that not everyone is privy to the same information and not everyone needs to be.

Not everyone has the same level of experience. Not everyone knows who the players are. And having everyone know all the details of every deal is only going to slow down the whole team by wasting team members' time on information that's not relevant to their tasks.

Want to screw over the managers who work for you? Then fill up their days with updates and demand to know exactly what is happening every moment of the day. If you keep too close tabs on your people, you'll communicate to the organization that you don't trust them to pass on information from below. You'll communicate that you think they're incapable of achieving their objectives by themselves. You'll communicate that they don't matter. And when you do that to the rest of your organization, congratulations—they won't matter.

The reason for adhering to the chain of command is not to keep some people in a substandard position and limit their chances for growth. It's to maximize the effectiveness of the team and allocate its resources properly. It's to ensure that all the team members know what they are doing, what their responsibilities are, and what the realistic expectations for success are.

If you want to create an effective chain of command, then do the following:

1. *Respect your own chain of command.* Your job is not about being popular. If you are, that's great. We all want a smile as we pass the receptionist's desk. But don't give people the idea that you're going to give someone preferential treatment. Communicate down through the ranks the same way you'd expect your people to communicate up to you. You can't yell and scream about how no one is following the chain of command when you're busy talking directly to the bottom floor.

2. *Reward and punish.* The only way to ensure that business is conducted properly without having to look at every detail is to enforce a chain of command by rewarding followers and punishing offenders. Don't kill communication in an effort to maintain control, but give your

people responsibility for what kind of information is passed along. A chain of command is not in place only to pass orders up and down. It is also used to pass information. And that means knowing what type of information is relevant at each level of your organization. The competition is about to launch a devastating new product—that's one thing. Ken just had a nice vacation—that's another. Ken needs to be told the rules if such an email goes companywide.

Your managers should realize that directors don't need to know every detail of an operation. Similarly, assistants don't need to know every detail of the annual budget. Giving people too much information bogs down the process, and the only way to maintain a proper flow is to reward those who work with it correctly and punish those who do not. Write down the offenders names. Have their bosses talk to them. Make it stick. If they don't get it, well, the option is yours. . . .

3. *Trust the people below you.* You should trust the people below you to pass your orders down effectively and to ensure that communication flows quickly and easily. Remember, having a structure does not mean that you have to have your fingers in everything. It means that you have a defined line of communication that ensures that you know just enough about what is going on to be able to direct it and step in when necessary. If a client calls, you want to know what is happening in general, and you want to know that what the client is interested in is being taken care of. You don't want, nor do you need, to know every detail. That would only clutter up your day and hold back your team from being effective.

4. If the people below you don't know what messages to pass on and what messages to hold onto, you need to train them. If the people below you can't do their work, that's another issue entirely. *Establish when it's okay to go around their boss.* Let your workers know that if they encounter incompetence, harassment, or illegal activities, they are to bring the issue up immediately with their direct superior. If that

goes nowhere, or if their immediate superior is party to the activity, then they are to move to the next senior in line. Still no result? Move up again. Let the workers know that managers who do not pass up critical information will be punished. But also let them know that bypassing their immediate boss is a personal indictment of their boss. In the end, therefore, either the boss will be in trouble for incompetence or criminality or the subordinate will be counseled for being wrong and bypassing his or her boss unnecessarily.

LESSON 7
BUILD BOUNDARIES TO PREVENT INFIGHTING AND CANNIBALISM

THE MISSION

The way SEAL teams are composed is designed to ensure that they make the most effective use of their firepower. Platoons have only 16 SEALs. This means that, at most, only 16 weapons are being fired at any one time. If too many SEALs are firing at the same target, this means that another potential target gets off lightly. For this reason, fields of fire and individual targets are designated. During an ambush, each target vehicle and individual is given to a specific gunner. Other gunners are assigned to cover flanks and the rear to guarantee protection. Still other SEALs are designated to sweep the entire area with fire to ensure redundancy.

Not assigning fields of fire invites disaster. A common assault tactic is to feint toward a target from one direction and attack from another. If you unload enough firepower from the initial direction, the enemy may think your feint is the actual attack and move defense forces in that direction. If the enemy hasn't assigned his people to cover permanent fields of fire, maybe all of the enemy will move, leaving the other sides exposed.

And that's when you win.

THE TAKE-AWAY

Have you ever seen a sales department? If it's good, the question is never "Can they sell?"—rather, the question is, "Where do you draw the lines on who sells what?" The issue should not be, "Do we have something that people want to buy?" Rather, it should be, "Who gets to sell which categories?"

This is not an unusual issue. It is something every sales department faces. And it's similar to selecting fields of fire for different team members. Think about it. You've got a bunch of Type A personalities with aggressive sales tendencies. They make their living through commissions and by beating their competition. Building a sales team is like throwing a bunch of starving people into a room with one slab of steak and one steak knife. If you don't define who gets what, everybody's going to lose.

When Jeff sets up a sales team, not only does he define sales categories for the team, but he also sets up a commission structure that encourages sharing ideas. Each of the salespeople makes a commission on his or her own sales, but bonuses are based on what the team as a whole accomplishes. That way, everyone has an incentive not only to work for him- or herself, but also to pass on information, ideas, and contacts to others. The goals should never be set just to specify who is able to sell to whom. But also to make sure that everybody knows the best way to sell whatever is created.

In setting up any team, you need to outline who is responsible for what, and where the lines are that can't be crossed. If you don't do this, you're guaranteeing infighting and cannibalization.

People worth their salt are going to be hungry for opportunities. Thus, you need to set boundaries so that everyone who is hungry can play. If people cross those lines, they'd better have a damned good reason. And no, being able to close a sale isn't a good enough reason for risking the good of the team. Nothing is.

LESSON 8
IF A MEETING IS GOING NOWHERE, KILL IT

THE MISSION

I recently watched a BUD/S class at the end of a long day. The students were lined up in boat crews, waiting for their leaders to finish their evening meeting. Some of the students swayed back and forth, ready to fall asleep. Others were staring angrily at the small conference that was going on. In front of them, the class leaders were laughing over what appeared to be personal jokes.

"This will change soon," I thought at the time. When things get tough enough, the evening meeting in front of the class will become a quick update. News will be given out to the guys. Then the guys will be cut loose. The leaders will huddle by themselves later if need be. But this class wasn't there yet. Its members would continue to suffer while their leaders fooled around in front of them.

THE TAKE-AWAY

If you haven't been in a bad meeting, you obviously haven't been working. We've both been to so many lousy wastes of time that we might as well have been on vacation. Meetings that lasted for hours and never accomplished anything. Meetings that digressed aimlessly and ended in a call for yet another meeting. Meetings that were rescheduled repeatedly for more than a month because nobody wanted to tackle the issues. Meetings that were simply vehicles to bully another team into submission.

We know we are not alone. And this is too bad because meetings are essential for bringing a team together and working through a project. Don't allow one to become just one more time killer in the business world.

If you're going to have a meeting, make sure it's treated like any other team activity. Make a plan and follow though. Ensure that a meeting is coordinated ahead of time, not during the meeting itself. Make sure you have a goal and make sure there is a leader. When you meet, you are coming together as a team. And just like a team, a meeting without leadership and goals is just going to be a big waste of resources, time, and effort.

When putting a meeting together, make sure you do the following:

• *Before the meeting.* Determine the objective of the meeting. Ensure that everyone knows what the meeting is for. Communicate the agenda and what everyone is expected to do to prepare. Let them know what they need to bring. Assign roles for the meeting. Who's the timekeeper? Who's presenting? Who's the "bad cop" to keep people on track?

• *During the meeting.* Begin by restating the rules. Go over the agenda. Define time limits. Once the meeting has begun, maintain the focus. Cut off people if they go off on a tangent. If something is important but not immediately relevant, discuss it outside the room. If the meeting becomes pointless, end it quickly and resolve to meet again *after* whatever issue on hand is taken care of. Do *not* waste people's time.

• *After the meeting.* Summarize what was accomplished. Define what has to be done. Assign individuals to specific tasks. Take down names and read them out loud so that everyone can hear.

• *Follow-up.* Send out a notice to all participants summarizing the meeting and reminding them of their commitments. If you don't do this, the meeting will soon be forgotten and you'll find yourself having the same meeting a few months later.

CHAPTER 3

LEADERSHIP
The Hardest Easy Thing

THE WAY IT IS

Who's leading your company? That's a fair question. After all, your department heads weren't born into the leadership positions they now hold. And we don't think there's an accredited university called Leadership U.

What if the people who are in charge of your company aren't leaders after all, and your company is rudderless? It could be that your product moved only because the economy has been kind. Or because that movie starlet happened to mention that she uses your brand. Or because your competitor is dealing with an embarrassing recall.

In the short run, this may be okay. In good times, organizations can run themselves for a while as long as enough bodies show up in the morning.

But what will happen next quarter when the world shifts? Who's going to keep you in business when a new competitor sees how soft you've become and lines up for a winner-take-all with you?

When that happens, can your vice president keep the troops motivated and engaged using the leadership tricks she picked up watching *Gladiator*? Will your project manager be able to push out the necessary changes in the line with that knee-jerk leadership technique he learned? You know—the one where he glares and gets defensive? Will the people who run your operations by screaming at people, who are already using hysteria as an incentive, be able to ramp up production even further? Will the hug-me touch-me players in your marketing division, who already have to beg their staffs to get through their normal workload, be able to ram better products through to the store shelves?

You're right. There's nothing to worry about. After all, your company has made a business out of handing out plaques, paperweights, and certificates to your employees with the word leadership on them. And a whole bunch of leadership inspirational posters hang in your hallways.

So business shouldn't be a problem when the world changes around you, right? Right?

The bottom line is, leadership is needed. Leadership aims the gun so that the teams can pull the trigger. If your leadership isn't stepping up and calling the shots, then your team is going to shoot the wrong guy. And you get only one shot.

LESSON 1
FORGET THE VILLAGE CONCEPT— ONE PERSON HAS TO BE IN CHARGE

THE MISSION

A few years ago, when I was going through advanced SEAL training, the instructors decided to enjoy themselves. It was dark out. We were past BUD/S, but we were still new to our teams. We had just arrived at our campsite. In a few hours, well before dawn, our training would begin. But before we could get our scant hours of sleep, two enormous 20-man tents had to be pitched. They were great, big, heavy canvas things, stuffed into great unwieldy bags along with their poles, but without instructions.

The instructors divided the class into two groups, enlisted men and officers, which was odd because enlisted men and officers go through SEAL training together. We stood around in our two groups. There were several officers in this class. We had all come in 2 years before, and we all had the same rank.

The instructors assigned each group to a tent, and the command master chief, the senior enlisted man in the training cadre, casually announced that he wanted to see which group could pitch its tent faster in the dark. There were no flashlights or campfires to be had. And, of course, we all knew that there was no such thing as a casual competition in the SEAL teams. Then, right before we started, the instructors took the officer group aside and confided in us that the organization had too many officers on board, and that they would be observing us very carefully to see who the real leaders were.

Then the competition began. The enlisted group moved like clockwork. They were all aware of who the senior petty officers were, and they immediately fell into work groups and began silently and efficiently erecting their tent. A second-class hull technician, probably 19 years old at the time, stood to one side, in charge of the situation on the other side of the clearing.

Our group of college-educated 20-something-year-olds immediately crowded into a circle. No one outranked the others, so we stood and first debated and then bickered over how we should get the job done. Finally, seeing that the other tent was halfway up, we fell upon our tent haphazardly, trying to catch up. To make matters worse, we all knew that the instructors were watching us, and as all of us were afraid that we might be pegged as having less leadership potential, we began strutting and shouting, as each of us was trying to appear as if he were in charge. One of the officers was loudly directing another how to hammer in a tent peg.

The instructors sat on one side, laughing.

THE TAKE-AWAY

Do you think this kind of thing doesn't happen in the business world? Think again. We've all walked into companies, divisions, and meetings where nobody's in charge. We've all labored under two or more managers, each of whom wants things done his or her way. And we've all seen the results: late hours, long days, poor results, and even poorer attitudes. Democracy doesn't work in the workplace. A designated leader does.

Why is this? To put it simply, someone has to be in charge. Someone has to make the difficult decisions that mean life or death for a company or project. Someone has to be able to take the blame when things go wrong, and to be there to redirect the resources and efforts to make them right. And if you think a committee of six or ten or twenty people can do this, just look at your own past and tell me how many times that's worked out well.

Organizations have been so busy touting their employees' leadership qualities, handing out leadership titles, and doling out leadership badges that leadership has become an entitlement. It's also become a curse to every manager who's actually supposed to lead. After all, if everyone's in charge at the same time, then no one's leading.

LESSON 2
STATE YOUR MISSION

THE MISSION

Before every operation, the SEAL mission commander stands up before his team. The doors are sealed, and a time check is taken—everyone synchronizes their dive watches. The team's mission is projected onto a screen, and the mission commander reads it loudly and articulately. It goes something like this:

> SEAL Team ONE FOXTROT will insert via submarine and conduct a hydro-reconnaissance of the northern beach on such and such an island, between the coordinates of X and Y.
>
> They will deliver the results to SEAL Team ONE Task Unit BRAVO via SATCOM by 0900 Zulu on 22 April 2003.

Everyone is asked whether there are any questions. Those questions that are asked are brief and to the point. Nobody tries to show how much additional information he knows. This is the time to ensure that one is on board, not to set oneself apart.

After the briefing, there is no misunderstanding about what the team's task is or what the mission commander expects. The commander has fully communicated what the team will do, how it will get there, and when things will happen. Everyone knows the criteria for success. There won't be any further questions about what is being attempted. Instead, everyone focuses on preparing dive and reconnaissance equipment, coordinating with the submarine, and planning insertion and extraction routes.

THE TAKE-AWAY

Have you been given a mission that sounds something like this: "Bill, Ms. Clark wants to drive new business. Can you go out and get some new clients?" If you have been given such a mission, you'd better work twice as hard at looking for that new job, because the job you have isn't just undefined, it's a no-win situation. What are your marching orders? Is your boss asking or directing you to do something? Is Ms. Clark looking for new business, or is she looking for a scapegoat in case new business doesn't come her way? And who is telling you what to do, anyway, Ms. Clark or your boss?

In this example, your boss is telling you his problem, and that's not the same as giving you a mission. When you only describe a problem, you open the door to many possible solutions. One of which might be: "Gone fishing. Tell Ms. Clark she can find her own new clients." There. That's a solution. It's probably not what the boss wants, however. But, it's an answer. Oh, well.

As a leader, communicating your mission means spelling out exactly what you want done, how you want it done, and how and when you want the results delivered. Doing this boldly and clearly reinforces the idea that you are in command, that you know what you're asking for, and that there is universal understanding of your task.

If you can't do this, then someone else is pointing the way.

LESSON 3
CHOOSE YOUR OPTION
WHILE THE CHOICE IS STILL YOURS

THE MISSION

Once, when I had been in the teams for a few years, I had a hard choice to make. I had been selected to go to freefall parachute school. That was a hard course to get into. Everyone wanted it, but everyone was always too busy to go. And then there were budget cuts that thinned the ranks out further. But I had just returned from a 6-month deployment to the Pacific and found my name on the top of the list. Then a major conflict began, and everyone was lining up outside the skipper's office trying to get in on that. And I got picked for that as well. So before the afternoon was over, I had to decide between learning how to freefall parachute and going to war.

In hindsight, my decision was obvious. I mean, like I was really going to choose going to freefall school over the chance to fight someone. But at the time, it seemed more difficult. The idea of jumping from an airplane over the warm Arizona desert, floating through the sky, and then softly landing in a drop zone the size of the southwest United States seemed really inviting. And, once more, I had just returned from a 6-month deployment.

What if I had taken a second too long to make my decision and my skipper had concluded that I wasn't a meat-eater? I'd have gone to freefall parachute school. That's something I still haven't done. It turned out to be the only opportunity to go that I had in my entire deployment-marked career. But if I had gone and I had missed out on a war, especially if I had gone as a result of hesitating, I would have cursed myself for the rest of my career.

What seemed like a difficult decision at the time was difficult only because a time limit was involved in the decision.

Suppose you're a SEAL platoon commander. You would be hard-pressed to put a limpet mine on a ship in Panama and put on a dog-and-pony show for a traveling congressional circus in San Diego on the same day, with only one squad. But the executive officer is soon going to have to write someone's name on the orders for travel to Panama. Which assignment do you want?

If you don't choose between the two missions early enough, you might miss out on Panama. You might end up fielding stupid questions instead of watching a ship blow up. Or, on the other hand, you might end up standing on the beach because you didn't have the boats you needed to go blow up the ship. Meanwhile, because you were standing and doing nothing on the Panamanian beach, you gave up an opportunity to gain additional funds from Congress. You let the team down because you were selfish for a mission. Or you might blow up the ship but lose one of your divers because your team wasn't ready for the mission.

But you don't have time to think. The executive officer has taken out his pen and is about to write down someone's name. Deep down inside, beyond the excitement and guilt and pressure, you know the answer that is most appropriate for you. Every SEAL knows the right answer to this one.

THE TAKE-AWAY

A few years ago, a small ad agency had a choice. It could spend a month working on a pitch for a $2 million piece of new business, or it could spend its time on a $100,000 project for an existing client. The managers knew that they didn't have the staff to do both.

But rather than make a choice, the leader tried to do both. He tried to shuffle people back and forth between working on the project and working on the pitch. He ended up doing both in a half-assed way. In the end, the client pulled the project and went with another agency, and the agency never had the time to do what it needed to do to make the pitch. In the end, it lost them both.

If you're waiting for the perfect option, you need to know that it's never going to come. If you're waiting for the time to be just right, it never will. If you're waiting for 100 percent, you're going to wait too long. And by then, the choice is no longer going to be yours. Your competition will jump into the opening, technology will offer new answers, or the opportunity may just fade away.

By hesitating, you're making a choice. You're choosing to take the decision out of your own hands and put it in the hands of someone else. And this means that you lose. Instead, decide what you want. You know the correct answer. Point the team in the right direction and go after it.

LESSON 4
STAND UP AND TAKE THE HIT

THE MISSION

On the very first day of SEAL basic training, a program called BUD/S, I got caught in the very first goon squad. That's what they call the group of students who can't hang on during the rope slide, who fail to perform endless repetitions of push-ups, or who straggle behind everyone else during a sand run. Everyone is struggling to get across the finish line, lungs about to explode, and suddenly an instructor will step out and raise his hand and all the stragglers get herded out into the sand. And then it's circus time.

The senior officer of the goon squad is supposed to step forward and lead the gaggle in whatever punishment the instructors have in store. And the whole group is supposed to be loud, screaming out the count as they do endless push-ups or eight-count body-builders—throwing it back in the instructors' faces as if nothing the instructors can throw at them will break them. The instructors want to see a unified gang of in-your-face resistance.

But on this first day, I was the senior officer of the goon squad, and I figured that my chances of survival would be better if I didn't draw attention to myself. What difference would it make who was up in front while we were doing push-ups, right? As a leader, I needed to be protected. That was reasonable. So, as the exhausted students gathered on the sand, I didn't step forward, but instead stayed in the background and let a second-class petty officer step forward instead.

The instructors went through one round of exercises, grilling and grinding the petty officer. They all fell into a steady tempo behind him. Then I sensed someone standing behind me, and a giant instructor put his paw on my shoulder. "Sir? Shouldn't you be up there?"

Even at that distance, you could see the crestfallen expression on the other men's faces as they stopped and stood watching. *The guy in charge is hiding in the back.* The instructors quickly dismissed the rest of the goon squad, and they straggled back to the main group, leaving me alone with the instructor.

He told me to kneel down and get in the push-up position again, and I did. "These men are looking for someone to lead them," he said simply, squatting next to me . "If you're not willing to lead them, don't waste their time." He was very professional, as if he was treating a sick patient. He continued to talk, waiting for my arms to begin to tremble. And then the circus began.

THE TAKE-AWAY

Have you seen what happens in a meeting when the client asks what went wrong and the manager points the finger at an employee? The client gets the distinct feeling that nobody's steering the ship, and the first question in her or his head is, "What the hell am I paying for?" As if that's not bad enough, the other members of the team are thinking to themselves, "Is that what's going to happen to me?"

You're a leader. Your people are watching you every time they see you. They're looking at every action, every moment. When they don't see you, they assume that you're working on their behalf. When they do see you, what you do confirms or destroys their assumptions.

If they see you take the hit, stand up for what's right, or go down fighting, they won't care whether you're dressed well or whether your grammar is correct. They'll swarm up in your defense, work overtime, and go the extra mile.

But if they see you shirk or run away, then they'll just work for wages. And they'll be gone as soon as a better offer comes along.

LESSON 5
MAKE A GODDAMNED DECISION

THE MISSION

My platoon trained for missions in a MOUT (Movement Over Urban Terrain) environment. During one training session, we stood just inside the tree line, watching the enormous mock city across the field in front of us. The city amounted to several tall buildings and a number of houses, together with winding streets and alleyways. We could do whatever we wanted in the facility. We could climb over and rappel off of the buildings. We could shoot our weapons at the soldiers who were acting at being our enemy.

Lasers were attached to our gun barrels, and we fired blanks. The concussions from our blank rounds initiated the lasers. If a laser hit one of the special vests everyone wore, the vest would ring with a loud, built-in alarm and the person hit would be considered dead and was supposed to drop. We also had simulated grenades, which amounted to grenades in which the normal charge had been replaced with what amounted to a firecracker. It was a great training facility.

In front of us, across the field, a few enemy soldiers had dug into a hardened position at the town's edge. They were buried deep inside the living room of a large concrete house. A ring of barbed wire surrounded the house. Within the living room, they had constructed a shelter out of sandbags against the wall opposite from the room's only window. They had cut a small opening in the side of the shelter that faced the window, just large enough to be able to stick a grenade launcher or gun barrel through. From inside the shelter, they could peer out and fire their machine guns and grenade launchers across the room, out the window, across the meadow, and into the U.S. convoy that would soon come into view. The convoy was racing to deliver ammunition to a besieged U.S. force a short distance away.

We tried moving around the tree line to get at the enemy's flank. But we couldn't do it. Other enemy gunners lay hidden in the town and fired on us as we moved around the side. In the meantime, we didn't have a sniper to shut down the soldiers in the shelter. The only way to stop them from killing the Americans in the convoy in just a few moments was to cross the field, climb over the barbed wire, climb in through the window, cross the room, and jam a grenade through the small opening so that it exploded among them.

During such an assault, we would all be under fire. Our only protection would be whatever suppression fire we shot back at them. At the same time, if we didn't do it, they could kill dozens of Americans in the convoy and stop supplies from getting to troops that badly needed them. What should we do?

I motioned for my point man to cautiously patrol near the house. He and his buddy were in the middle of the field when machine-gun fire erupted from the building. It was too late to decide! Another enemy machine gun opened up on us from a rooftop. I yelled for everyone to assault the building. All 16 of us began sprinting toward the building in two parallel lines so that only two people would be exposed to the machine gun at once. Alarms starting going off and the two SEALs in front dropped. Then another SEAL dropped. But the SEAL in the front of the other line reached the barbed wire cutting across the field and flung himself on it, crushing the loops down beneath his body. Those of us who remained trampled over his body, clearing the wire. The other line hesitated, then spread out and began firing back at the machine gun. Two of them went down, but the machine-gun fire from the house died abruptly. It then restarted, but by then we were at the house.

I got to the window first and knelt down on hands and knees, and the SEAL behind me leaped up on my back and lunged through the window into the machine-gun fire. I could hear his alarm going off immediately, but another SEAL was right behind him, and then another. Meanwhile, another SEAL was firing continuously into the room. I leapt up and climbed into the room, and my alarm went off immediately. I dropped and saw another SEAL crouching against the bomb shelter, below the small opening. Alarms were going off within the shelter and someone was clamoring to take up the machine gun. The crouching SEAL reached up, stuck his hand through the opening and dropped a simulated grenade. It went off, and the exercise was over. We had suffered nine casualties, over half the platoon.

MOUT instructors teach this scenario to emphasize a point: When you are out in the open and you come under attack, you have to act immediately. You're going to be cut down in seconds. Moreover, you can be shot in the back running away just as easily as you can be shot in the front running forward. So, if you don't have time to fully assess the situation and you have to move immediately, you should automatically charge forward. That way, you can at least fire back as you run.

Every additional second you take to reach this conclusion on your own, for the second time, means wasted lives. In the time it takes you to read this sentence, someone else on your team will die. The key to survival is simply your making a decision to move. Just give an order. Just tell them to move!

THE TAKE-AWAY

His name was Jim, but we called him the flag. Why? Because he never made a decision. He just blew in the direction of the prevailing wind. So we did what everyone else did: We included him in the meetings because of his title, but none of us ever paid any attention to him, and none of us ever relied on him. Why? Because he never stood up and took the lead.

If you're in charge, people need to know that you're in charge. The only way they know is by watching you make decisions. And if you don't do that job, then someone else will. And that person will be the leader everyone follows from then on, regardless of his or her rank or title.

Are you waiting until you have all the information? You're never going to get it. Are you waiting to weigh all the options? By the time you figure them all out, the first option will have changed, and you're back to the drawing board. Are you waiting for a sign? Are you waiting because you're scared? That's part of the job—it's never going to change.

A few years ago, a border war between Ecuador and Peru threatened to spill over into neighboring countries, wreck the regional economy, and damage the regional democratic process. Jon and another SEAL, along with a group of Special Forces and a group of commandos from several South American countries, were inserted into the upper Amazon to monitor how the war was progressing. They operated out of a central base camp and rotated through small outposts in the jungle. A young American linguist who was not a commando was also on their team. They always placed him at what they thought were the safest locations.

One rainy evening, everyone was at the base camp except the linguist and a senior commander from one of the South American militaries. Another SEAL was monitoring the radio. Suddenly, the linguist's voice came over the radio. It was obvious that he was afraid. You could almost hear him swallow.

"We're under attack," he reported. You could hear gunfire in the background. You could hear the frog in his throat as he relayed his situation. "What should we do?" The SEAL told him to get down on his stomach and to crawl out of the camp in a particular direction until he could hide in the surrounding jungle. "Crawl?" You could hear his companion, the outraged senior officer from South America, in the background. "I will not crawl in the mud!"

"Maybe we should just wait here?" the linguist asked over the radio. The terror in his voice was obvious. "I don't think the commander wants to move." The other SEAL tried reasoning and arguing with them to move, to no avail. "I don't know what to do," the linguist said at last.

Suddenly a large explosion was heard in the immediate background.

"We're on the way!" the senior officer yelled out in the background. A few seconds later, they were crawling through the mud, dragging the radio behind them.

They had hesitated out of fear. Something that paralyzed them from making a decision. The thought of making a mistake prevented them from acting. And had they remained paralyzed, the next mortar round might have landed on them.

In another instance, Jon had a SEAL instructor once who, during an operation in Latin America, was patrolling across a small dirt road with his platoon. Suddenly, a few hundred yards down the road, an enemy platoon began to cross the road in the opposite direction. The SEAL instructor sank down and froze in the middle of the road. For the next few moments, not wanting to move to one side or another, he waited, out there in the open, until the enemy platoon crossed and disappeared.

Deciding not to move because it's the best choice is not the same thing as doing nothing out of fear. It's still a decision. How do you reach such a decision? Try to anticipate these situations. Make the decision before the situation actually happens. Then, when the situation does happen, remember what you had already decided to do. And trust that what you had previously decided to do was correct.

Jon's platoon was practicing being hunted through the swamps while rescuing downed pilots. It had just located the downed pilots lying behind several knocked-down trees beside a major path. As the platoon approached, its rear security suddenly signaled, and the men all froze and then got down. Jon and several other members of the platoon were in the open on the path.

After a few seconds, the point man from one of the units hunting for us suddenly barged through the bushes. He stood on the path and waited, smoking a cigarette. A minute went by. They were all right around him. Another minute went by. He looked at one of Jon's heavy weapons gunners, who was sprawled on the ground, completely exposed like Jon, nearby. Their eyes met, and he looked at his machine gun. Jon knew what he was thinking: They could take out this one guy. But other bad guys were undoubtedly nearby. Then they would be all over them. The story of the BUD/S instructor who had been in Latin America flashed in Jon's mind. He slowly rolled his eyes back and forth so his heavy weapons gunner could see. The gunner slightly lowered his chin in a nod. Another long minute went by. Then the enemy soldier barged off into the bushes again.

Remember, the fear that's preventing you from making a decision during a stressful situation is often simply the result of an assumption that you're going to make things worse by acting. But something bad is already happening. *The printer needs to know the color we want, now! Or else the price doubles!* Anticipate these situations. Recognize, ahead of time, that you will have to make a decision. Then make it. You'll be surprised at how well it turns out.

LESSON 6
PUT YOUR STAMP ON THINGS RIGHT AWAY

THE MISSION
We once had a new commander who took his time making his mark. He sat in his office, apparently deliberating over reports and making plans. Weeks went by. The team was solid already, so his absence did not appear to the troops to be a bad thing. It was seen as an endorsement of the way things were being run already. It was seen as confirmation of the way the previous skipper had run things.

That made this new commander a sort of caretaker skipper. His job was simply to maintain what he had inherited. Patch things up as they wore out. Just keep the boat that someone else had built afloat.

Of course, some of the more seasoned team members had a less rosy opinion. "There's a rumor that we have a new skipper," one of them remarked. "Of course, I could be wrong. But I know I saw *somebody* in the skipper's office."

THE TAKE-AWAY
He's the ghost in the machine. He's the wizard behind the curtain pulling the strings. He's the one behind the scenes running the show. That mysterious figure whom we never see, but whom we assume controls it all.

We all have a tendency to assume someone is manipulating the situation, no matter how chaotic the situation actually is. Someone in HR is looking out for my career. Someone in sales is talking to the trade about our lost shelf space. Someone in R&D is building something in response to that new competitive product.

The truth is, if you don't see leadership, it probably doesn't exist. If you don't know about your department's promotions plan, there may not be one. If you haven't spoken with HR, they may not know you exist, let alone care about your future. We don't know about you, but the only time we've seen a successful operation is when whoever took charge did so in a way that everyone knew about it. They led from in front of the briefing room, or through email, or from the back of the squad, but everyone knew they were there. Maintaining the status quo may be the marching orders, but it's still the orders. Do something so that people know you're the one who issues them. Make a public announcement. Send out a universal email. Go around and shake everyone's hand. Pick at least one small objective, and tell everyone that you, as a team, will accomplish it. Do something!

If you don't, you risk being passed by. The world moves quickly. The current status quo can soon become a thing of the past. New events and new problem-solvers will arise. And then you'll be swept out of office, along with the other garbage, ghosts, and antiques.

LESSON 7
GIVE THEM THE BIG PICTURE

THE MISSION

After spending several weeks bobbing around in rough seas with no smuggler vessel in sight, it was hard to remember that our team was contributing to the war against weapons of mass destruction. Every day, the boat crews clandestinely moved down to the water and launched their boats for the long transit. The reconnaissance teams spent hours infiltrating to their positions, and then they sat and stared through night vision devices. Interception team members spent their nights balancing on small boats, breathing diesel fumes, and getting soaked. In the morning, everyone straggled in and got a few hours of sleep. Then the cycle was repeated. It would have been easy to reach the burnout threshold after a week or two, with no target vessels yet discovered, let alone taken down.

It was important that the guys knew why they were doing this. They had to know that countries were smuggling seemingly harmless materials like oil and dates in order to finance their purchase of ballistic missile components, ex-Soviet physicists, and high-grade plutonium. They had to know that even if they didn't capture a smuggler, but the operation deterred the movement of materials in one direction or the movement of weapons in the other, then they had succeeded.

Deterring a potential smuggler isn't as satisfying as climbing over a gunwale and taking down the crew of a ship that's full of contraband, but it still counts. The rogue country has that much less money to finance its military. It's important that the team knows this. The team will have prevented an enemy nation from purchasing tanks and missiles, which is the same as destroying those weapons later on.

THE TAKE-AWAY

Picture this —a team of 40 people working in an ad agency. The creatives are some of the brightest and most driven people you've ever worked with. But unless they understand the big picture, they will produce some of the most fabulous, unique, and completely irrelevant advertising art around.

Paying for a television commercial that wins awards but fails to drive sales or build the brand is a mistake that costs millions of dollars. Something didn't happen right—the results. And it's usually not because the creatives weren't talented or the account director wasn't a visionary. More likely, the big-picture objective was forgotten in the process. Somewhere, someone produced a gorgeous picture that didn't support the take-away– the company's profits.

People generally don't enjoy working in the dark. After all, you don't. If the only view someone has of the company is the four walls of their cube or office, then that's the extent of their concerns. If they know they're a part of something bigger, if they know how much their work matters and how it fits into the big picture, they're going to treat their work accordingly.

LESSON 8
POINT THE BOAT IN THE RIGHT DIRECTION

THE MISSION

When a new skipper comes on board a SEAL team, he puts out his message fast. A few weeks into my first assignment to a team that specialized in driving miniature submarines, we had a change of command. At the time, the team was already an outstanding place to work. The diving was great. New subs were coming on line. The technicians were extremely qualified. There was a great balance between hard work and hard play.

Nevertheless, the new commanding officer wasted little time in making some changes. He called all the team members into the large bay area where we staged the mini-subs and put out the new word. But what he put out wasn't universally well received. He said he was going to try to move the team to Seattle, where the water was always colder. We were in sunny San Diego at the time. You could hear a pin drop.

He said he wanted us to train like we'd fight. Since we were up against the Soviet Union, we'd start training as if we were in the Soviet Union. That meant cold water. Our dives would be longer. We'd experiment with new equipment, new foods, and new medical techniques that might extend the length of time we could operate in frigid water. We'd wear wet suits as well as dry suits, determining how long we could remain submerged with cold water directly against our skin. We'd have cranes ready to hoist swimmers out if they could no longer move their limbs after extended operations.

I imagined the stampede of people to the detailer as they tried to get their orders changed—and away from that team.

Two years later, the command was still an exceptional place to work, maybe even more exceptional. The resident commandos were fired up. The technicians had worked on things that had never been tried before, in places that they had never expected to deploy to. That the entire team never permanently moved to Seattle made little difference. Every platoon had conducted extensive cold-water training. Everyone knew that the commander focused on what was operationally sound. The mini-subs were successfully used in combat operations. A stronger collective attitude pervaded the team, the attitude that we would go anywhere and do anything to achieve our mission.

THE TAKE-AWAY

You can paddle as hard as you want and you can make sure everyone's daiquiri glass is full, but if the boat isn't pointed in the right direction, you could end up like Gilligan, lost at sea. Many a manager has claimed, as he or she was shown the door, "But I ran the division on 12-hour shifts and 7-day weeks." Too bad they were all making the wrong product.

Jeff worked for a company where a long-standing cash cow had to give way to a promising new product. The existing product had been one of the greatest launches the company had ever conducted. Consumers still wanted it, and sales remained strong. It received a good portion of the company's advertising and promotions budget.

But the market was changing. Consumers were becoming more sophisticated. Although they were currently happy with the existing product, tests indicated that the new product satisfied some of their needs even further. It was time to turn the boat.

Not everyone was convinced. Getting an organization turned toward the right direction means making some tough decisions. It often means changing the way things are done and the way people think. Change is never a comfortable thing, and people will feel threatened. Many workers associate their careers with the existing product. The idea of siphoning off advertising dollars to the new product makes workers uneasy.

The fact is, you will almost never be able to satisfy everyone. You will be blamed for your decisions because people who are currently benefiting are going to see their fortunes change. But since change is inevitable, you're stuck with it. The whole thing is going to come crashing down sooner or later. The only thing you can do is attempt to have some degree of influence over the change. So get over worrying about making some people unhappy. Instead of focusing solely on the problems that come with change, focus on where you want to go and how to get people on board. Sure you're going to lose a few on the way. But they're lost already. There are others out there who will be attracted to the new direction, as long as you point out what that direction is and explain what's at the end of the journey.

LESSON 9
GET COMFORTABLE WITH CHAOS

THE MISSION

SEALs plan the hell out of every mission and then anticipate that at some point during the mission they will nonetheless have to depart from their plan. They plan exhaustively in order to remove as many unknown variables as possible, but there are always more. SEALs bring an extra outboard motor in case of catastrophic engine failure. They plan for the possibility of being discovered by enemy guards, and of becoming separated from one another en route to their objective. Mission planning resembles a continually forking tree branch, with every fork representing several possible contingencies.

At the same time, SEALs know that they can't anticipate everything. There are too many variables. Something unanticipated will happen during the parachute jump, or the patrol, or the demolition raid that will force the platoon to respond and perhaps deviate from the original plan. To overcome such unknowns, SEALs apply serious creative problem solving and bring lots of weapons to fight their way out if need be. They carry large amounts of extra gear, maintain a versatile organizational structure, and embrace unconventional approaches to finding a solution. To train for this, SEAL exercises are never scripted events in which the platoon knows everything it will encounter ahead of time. SEAL teams promote a culture that thrives on chaos and that pushes through to success no matter what is unexpectedly encountered.

"That is why, if there had been a war between the United States and the Soviet Union, you would have won."

That statement was made by a former member of a Soviet commando team. I was talking to him in the Baltics after the fall of the Berlin Wall. We were comparing notes on planning techniques. He had already been allowed to observe a NATO planning exercise, and he had been amazed by the degree to which the Americans and British were forced to muddle through new situations, work with incomplete information, and command unreliable forces. It was a very different approach from the carefully scripted exercises that had been conducted by members of the Warsaw Pact.

During the NATO exercise, he said, the exercise commander was cursing and the intelligence chief was screaming into the telephone. "It was chaos," he said. "Everybody was trying to figure out what was going on. But since war is chaos, you would win, because you apparently operate like that normally."

THE TAKE-AWAY

Say you've got one team building a Web site for a client, another team integrating an online marketing program into an offline campaign, and yet another team launching a new product. You're heading up a research project for another client, and oh, by the way, you're also working on two pitches for new business. One of the creative people has just quit because his rock band is touring in Europe for 2 months. And now one of the companies you pitched several months ago is ready to start its project and wants to launch it in 2 weeks.

And this is called success? You bet.

Along the way, the deadlines change, the designs change, the technologies change, and the budgets change.

And this is called progress? Damned right.

Change is part of the deal. Change is part of success. You'd better be ready for it or you're going to fall behind. Because every time there's a change, there's a degree of chaos. People don't know what to do; people don't know how to integrate new ideas, concepts, demands, or tools.

Can you accurately predict what's going to happen? Not always. Will you know ahead of time which response will work? Rarely. All you can predict for sure is that there is going to be change. All you know for sure is that some kind of response will be required. Invest in a flexible organization that can adapt and provide the right solution.

Commando organizations have done this since they were created. Following the Iranian hostage disaster in 1980 ("I think we have an abort situation"), the Special Operations Command was formed, combining commando organizations from the Navy, Army, and Air Force. SEAL task units, which combine several SEAL platoons with a command and control element, were promoted when it became clear that evolving situations required larger commando responses than a single platoon could realistically handle. With the beginning of the new century, the SEAL organization has reorganized itself again, placing greater emphasis on command mobility, team integrity, and operational versatility.

The people who are successful are those who can adapt to new business environments, new business demands, and new business needs. Those who can handle chaos survive. Those who can't, don't.

LESSON 10
THE VAST MAJORITY OF THE TIME, YOU KNOW WHAT YOU SHOULD DO

THE MISSION

During a month of jungle training, my platoon was given the task of taking down an enemy encampment in the middle of a swamp during daylight hours. The encampment itself was located at the end of a thin spit of land that rose up a foot or so from the surrounding morass and was bordered on all three sides by a dark, serpentine stream. The spit of land was too thin to allow us to bring our entire platoon on line, which would have enabled us to bring all of our weapons to bear at one time. At the same time, the enemy would expect that any assault would come from the other end of the spit, as that was the most obvious avenue of approach. Most of their guards had probably already been given instructions to fire in that direction.

The solution to assaulting the encampment, therefore, lay in convincing the enemy that an assault was coming from another direction, so that they would turn their weapons away from down the spit and thus allow an assault force to approach from the now unguarded direction. That meant that we had to create a diversionary attack from some other direction out in the swamp. Then, when the actual assault began, the diversionary assault team would have to lay down fire just ahead of the assault team advancing down the spit, and guide the assault team into the enemy camp.

The problem was that whoever conducted the diversionary attack had to do so from far out in the swamp. It had to appear as if the assault were coming from somewhere completely other than the spit. The swamp, meanwhile, was made up of dark, waist-deep water inhabited by mosquitoes that seemed large enough to carry off small children. Additionally, the area was home to alligators, snapping turtles that could bite off the end of your boot and several toes, and several kinds of poisonous snakes. To get into position far away from the spit would take hours of slow movement, low down in the muck to avoid being spotted. Once they got into position, the diversionary team would have to lie there in the muck until the time for the assault arrived. The diversionary team would then have to link up with the actual assault team by quickly crossing more swamp and then the stream, which was of unknown depth. The success of the diversionary team was essential to the success of the mission.

Meanwhile, there were several other reasons to avoid being on the diversionary team. The clothes we had on were the clothes we would wear for the next few days, so whoever was on the diversionary team would sleep and eat wet during that time. Moreover, as platoon commander, I was traditionally a member of the main assault team. Would the rest of the team think I was less of a leader if I did not take that position? Would they assume that I had given up control of the platoon? How could I be off running a side operation that was out of sight, and yet still be clearly be in charge of the platoon?

So there it was. Should I lead the diversionary team and ensure that it succeeded, or should I stay dry and lead the main assault team? Was there really any question?

THE TAKE-AWAY

You know what to do. Times are tough. Business has ground to a halt, the economy is in the dirt, companies are laying off people, and the country is embroiled in defending itself against a half-hidden enemy. Upper management has put out that earnings will be flat for several quarters to come. In this situation, it's tempting to lay low, stay with the herd, and not cause problems.

Then you analyze data and conclude that things are even worse. Profits aren't flat. Expenses actually far exceed revenues. This is a public company. If you start reporting big losses, the stock is going to plummet and the whole thing will collapse. You can save the company by cutting back expenses so that they're in line with the fallen revenues, but that's going to mean letting people go.

On paper, it's real easy: You cut a few people with the stroke of your pen to save the company. In reality, it's far tougher. You're going to have people you see every day suddenly without jobs. You're going to rip apart the family that you created. You're going to get rid of the guy who coaches your daughter's soccer team. When people claim that they don't know what to do, most of the time what they mean is, they want someone to get them off the hook. People know what the right thing to do is, whether it's laying people off to save a company, firing one person because he or she is bringing the group down, infiltrating through ice-cold water and a 12-foot surf zone to ensure a mission's success, or turning down a gift from a subordinate. These are all no-brainers. You know what to do.

The problem is with all the other stuff. Reconciling yourself with the reality of what has to happen. Anticipating the discomfort, hardships, and conflicts you'll cause by doing the right thing. *"But, honey, they've had us over for dinner."*

We wish there were an easy answer for that, but there isn't. It's the hardest part of making a tough decision. But that should never stand in the way of making the right decision. Be the hard boss. Be strong. That's your job.

LESSON 11
IF YOU THINK NO ONE ELSE CAN REPLACE YOU, YOU'RE AN EGOTISTICAL S.O.B. WHO'S FAILED

THE MISSION

My platoon was in the Nevada desert, practicing the rescue of downed pilots in anticipation of future operations. We were into our second week. Every night, we had been flown out by a helicopter that followed the contours of the earth and darted around simulated surface-to-air missile sites. The pilots dropped us off in the darkness and then sped home. Then we proceeded on foot for miles toward the place where the downed pilot was hiding or running or in captivity.

On this particular night, the trainers pitted our SEAL platoon against another platoon. We both had the same launch time and were the same patrol distance from where the pilots were last reported. The first platoon to get airborne again, with the rescued pilot, would win.

The platoon we were up against was confident and fit. Its equipment was better than ours. Each member had new GPS devices and communications gear. Earlier, when we had met and they had shown us their stuff, one of my platoon members had asked, "How'd you get equipment like this?" "Because our platoon gets real missions," their platoon commander replied. Then he was off, yelling at his guys, telling everyone what to do. His chief and leading petty officer stood quietly to one side as he hustled around, doing everything.

That evening, we were inserted on the side of a sand dune. We quickly formed a perimeter, waved off the helicopters, and began a quick patrol toward our first rally point. After a few thousand yards, I called a halt. My assistant platoon commander had a great idea: He and I informed the rest of the platoon that we had just suffered brain aneurysms and were incapable of making any further decisions. Whether the platoon succeeded or not that night would depend on the rest of the crew.

It wasn't an unusual situation for a SEAL platoon. Everyone in the platoon was familiar with every platoon operation. My assistant platoon commander could have immediately jumped into my spot. The chief could have successfully rammed home any operation. And he could have been ably replaced by the leading petty officer. This move was simply another chance for the guys to prove that they could step forward.

The assistant platoon commander and I moved to the side and watched the remaining guys huddle briefly. Then they were off. A few hours later, as we rode back through the canyons with the rescued pilot, we were able to pick up radio transmissions from the other platoon, which was still on the ground. The platoon commander was still yelling at his guys. They were obviously useless without his expert guidance.

THE TAKE-AWAY

You're the person in charge. You're responsible for leading the group below you, and everyone in the company knows that no decision is made without your nod. You're indispensable to the company because without you, your group isn't going to function. And that makes you secure. It should. Because you're essential to the operation.

So let me ask you, what happens when you want to go on vacation? What happens when you're sick? Five years from now, when you're still running the same group and watching other people get promoted, are you going to wonder why? Or are you still going to be happy that you're indispensable? After all, the company knows that without you in that position, things aren't going to work right.

It's great to have a fiefdom to control. But if controlling it means locking yourself up in a castle while the world spins past you, then pretty soon that's all you're going to have. And you're going to have to run it 24/7/365. Congratulations.

There's a price for that kind of security—the growth of the rest of the organization.

Real security lies in developing your backup, in building a team below you that can function without you, so that you can look for new opportunities and growth. If you keep growing, there won't be a person out there who'll be able to pull the rug out from under you. And that's real security.

LESSON 12
THERE'S NO "I" IN
"SHUT UP AND DO THE WORK"

THE MISSION

During an operation in the Middle East, the task unit I was part of received a warning order to prepare for an urban building assault. There wasn't much time to plan. A helicopter was being spun up. The only way to get down to the building was by fast-roping. That is, the assault team would quickly slide down ropes from hovering helicopters to the rooftops, the same way firemen slide down poles at the fire station.

A member of the support team was concerned. "We need to make sure the platoon has all the qualifications to do this," he said. "You know, the right rope and the right training."

The task unit commander had been an enlisted man prior to receiving his commission, and he had a zillion years of experience. The clock was ticking. "What?" he asked, thrusting an imaginary rope at the support officer. "Here's a rope. Slide down it."

A few weeks later, there was a similar situation. We were on board a vessel operated by resistance fighters, reconnoitering enemy waters, when someone spotted a mine in the water. It was close to the vessel—20 feet off. A thousand pounds of high explosive that would detonate if it simply rubbed up against the hull.

There was a rapid debate about how to destroy the mine as it bobbed closer. Then the task unit commander's hand went up. Silence. "That's enough. Get over there. Punch a hole in the side of the thing and sink it right now."

End of story.

THE TAKE-AWAY

In the end, someone's got to do the work. Don't get us wrong—being able to sit back and generate ideas is great. It's something we all like to do. Hell, we'd both love jobs where the only measure of our success was how many new ideas we came up with. But unfortunately, someone's got to turn those ideas into profits, and that takes work.

In the late 1990s, a high-tech consultant whom we know was involved in starting up a microchip factory abroad. During one interview, while he was looking for talent to operate the factory, he asked a management candidate what he could offer. Unfortunately, the candidate said that he was really more of a strategic thinker—a big-picture person who was best suited for conceptualizing ideas and coming up with plans. The consultant looked him in the eyes and said simply, "Understand one thing. There is only one big-picture person here, and that's me. I'm looking for people who can take our objectives and implement solutions to meet them."

Leading is not just about seeing an opportunity; it's also about taking the resources at hand and turning that opportunity into something real. Microsoft would have been nothing if Bill Gates had stopped at his idea for an operating system and hadn't actually built it. Jerry Bruckheimer is a leader in Hollywood because he can develop a new idea into a box office hit and do it again, and again, and again.

Yes, part of being a leader is generating ideas. But it's more about being able to say, "Enough ideas. Now shut up and do the work."

LESSON 13
DON'T BECOME ONE OF THE FOLLOWING STEREOTYPES

THE MISSION AND THE TAKE-AWAY

There are times, although rare, when screaming is effective. There are times when it pays to step back and watch the show run itself. But if you do either of these things too often, your team will anticipate your style, and then bad things will happen. Use the following techniques occasionally, but don't become known for one of them.

The Volcano

One of the teams had a skipper once who turned out to be a screamer. He was a good man who knew his business. He could make things happen fast. Put him in a firefight, and he'd have us kicking ass. He could walk into an admiral's office and browbeat him into giving us a mission. But he had a habit of massacring the messenger as well. There were stories about him publicly humiliating his men during quarters. Stories about him going totally ape when things didn't go as planned. Stories about how, when he tried to bulldoze a bad plan through, it stank for everyone—like the toasted guy in my BUD/S class who led a charge into simulated enemy machine-gun fire. Team members tried to jump ship to other teams. No one wanted to extend their stay under him.

The Country Club Manager

It's most often young SEAL officers who make this mistake. They're new to the team. They want to belong to the club. They know that their fate rests with gaining their team's support. They become too familiar, letting the guys out of assignments, calling guys by their nicknames before they've earned the right to do so. In short, they seek to become a friend and not learn the ropes the hard way.

Jon had an officer like that in advanced training. He never demanded a lot from the guys. And they were good at thinking up creative, imaginative contingency solutions. But then it caught up with him. A few of the guys went along with his pretenses and treated him like their buddy. Then the day came when he really did have to lay down the law. His men saw him as a S.O.B. for suddenly doing this, after pretending for so long that he was their friend. They resisted his demands, which he saw as abandonment. He took it really personally, given how leniently he had treated them. In the end, his training squad was ineffective during tough situations, and he wasn't given a platoon. When he complained about this, the team skipper replied, "Well, you could always resign."

The Bank Manager

There are times when it is necessary to stay fastidiously within precise boundaries and faithfully adhere to established procedures. Keeping track of classified cryptography depends on detailed record keeping and thorough destruction procedures. Extracting eight commandos by fastening their harnesses to a strong rope that's fastened to an ascending helicopter requires the same attention to detail to make sure nothing and no one slips, drops, breaks or falls.

Alternatively, commando warfare, by definition, inherently requires new and special ways of conducting business. Rubber boats that can be parachuted out of aircraft, 50-caliber sniper rifles, and specially outfitted dune buggies wouldn't be available if commandos hadn't pushed the envelope. As once-special tactics and equipment become conventional, it's necessary to create new tactics and equipment to provide a continual edge.

Moreover, when a commando team is assigned a mission, it's necessary to change from administrative rules to operational rules. Safety gives way to operational necessity. It might actually be necessary to drive that miniature submarine through waters that the crew has never navigated before. The bank manager who can't make this transition ensures that the teams he commands will be only as capable as they are now. A predilection to avoid risks will keep your team safe and ensure that all the bullets are accounted for, but your operators will hate you because you'll prevent them from being employed. As they say, a battleship is safe in a harbor, but that's not the job of a battleship.

The Manager Who Can't Be Satisfied

He or she comes into your office near closing time, glares at you, and announces that an additional project has to be completed before morning. But it's almost six. . . . Your boss continues to glare at you. You imagine your family sitting down for dinner together. He or she continues to glare. In the end, you acquiesce, and make the sacrifice. "Something important came up," you say on the phone when you call home.

The next morning you deliver the project to your boss. He or she simply grunts and turns back to the computer. You feel miffed. That evening, another extra project comes up. And the glare until you take it. You put out again. You receive another grunt the next morning. After a few more identical nights, you realize that what used to be considered an extra work load is now the standard. Only your boss isn't any happier. And then a project for the weekend comes. He or she glares and holds out the assignment until you take it.

At first, you fear that your boss believes you are an underperformer and is testing you. You decide to impress your boss and work twice as hard. You dedicate your weekend to the project and on Monday, you turn in an exceptional product. You receive another grunt. That evening, your boss glares at you while holding out another assignment.

"To hell with this," you decide. When your boss leaves, you call a headhunter.

The Cowboy

Neither of us knows if such a thing has ever been tolerated in modern commando teams. Yes, sometimes you need to charge forward. But, there are simply too many potential casualties and too much political currency resting on commando missions to entrust one to a cowboy. Authorization for an operation depends on the accurate calculation of operational risk. This requires an assessment of proven forces' ability to perform a task. All this is contrary to the cowboy philosophy of depending on experimentation, pluck, and luck in order to succeed.

Jon never encountered any cowboys in the SEAL teams. The closest to a cowboy he ever saw was a task unit commander whose boss referred to him as the Lone Ranger. When this task unit commander's name came up in conversation, his boss would press a button on his computer: The Lone Ranger theme would begin and a picture of the masked avenger would appear on the computer screen. That was because this task unit commander had pushed some ideas about assaults on the local admiral without consulting his boss first.

The guys love leaders who do stuff like that. They see them as hard-chargers who are willing to cut through the bullshit to make things happen. And it sometimes works. Jon had a boat detachment chief in the Arabian Gulf who plowed through to a solution for quickly transporting his vessels, using a foreign helicopter and an ad hoc rig. There was nothing in Navy regulations about doing it that way. It saved the task unit lots of time and effort. And he kept Jon informed.

The problem with being a cowboy is that your bosses won't employ you if they can't trust you, and they can't trust you if they don't know what you'll do. And then you're stuck with the reputation.

LESSON 14
KNOW WHICH LEADERSHIP STYLE TO USE

THE MISSION

During a jungle warfare mission, I used several different leadership styles. I took a step back during mission conception, when I wanted to encourage a creative environment and allow my platoon free rein to come up with possible solutions. Then I was the bank manager during mission planning and preparation, imposing strict controls to ensure that unnecessary risks were avoided. Then I was a cowboy right before the parachute jump as the adrenaline got going. Once, after another mission, I was the volcano, because we had screwed up badly and I wanted to ensure that it never happened again.

THE TAKE-AWAY

The key to being a leader is knowing when to turn up the heat and when to keep things at a slow simmer. You always need to keep the pressure on, but at different levels.

If you're negotiating, you may not want to hit someone with a 20-ton brick if you're not in a power position. You need to finesse the situation. If you need something done immediately, you may need to turn on the volcano and make it happen. If you're mired and nobody can move, it's time to open the gates and let the cowboy take charge. And if you're coming into budget season and you need to dot every I and cross every T, then you need to play the role of the bank manager.

Learning what to do when requires watching others in a variety of situations, observing what works and what doesn't, and then reading your people before you make a move. It's not about hesitating; it's about analyzing the situation. You don't want to rush in without knowing the game. You don't want to resort to using the same technique time after time, even if the situation has changed. If you do that, nine times out of ten, you'll do the wrong thing. The volcano won't promote creativity, and the country club manager won't promote immediate results.

LESSON 15
ENSURE THAT YOU POSSESS
THE THREE PRIMARY LEADERSHIP TOOLS

THE MISSION AND THE TAKE-AWAY

SEALs need three things in order to lead. Without them, leadership would be unenforceable, unfocused, or irresponsible.

Responsibility

A SEAL leader needs a mission. A SEAL platoon needs a mission. The best way to destroy a team of well-trained commandos is to put them behind a barbed wire stockade where they'll be perfectly safe and let them stew with nothing to do.

Working a mission is more than just taking action. It is taking responsibility for success. Unfortunately, this maxim is still too often ignored. A platoon that is stuck on Guam for 6 months begins to linger and grow fat. Time on the shooting range decreases. Qualifications in diving and parachuting begin to lapse. There is little incentive to train hard. No precedents and traditions for future operations are created. The team will die.

Authority

A SEAL leader needs the tools to complete his mission. He needs to be officially designated as the leader to ensure that he can exercise control. He must have the power to make decisions in the field if he is to overcome obstacles and solve problems.

If a SEAL leader is responsible for conducting a photo-reconnaissance mission, then he needs control over a reconnaissance-capable team. He needs the power to obtain and use cameras and data-relay equipment. He requires the power to obtain helicopters or boats to insert and extract his force. Without authority, he is at the mercy of the troops he is supposed to lead and the support elements whose aid he requires. He is reduced to being a beggar.

Accountability

There must be consequences for a SEAL leader who does not perform at an acceptable level. Performance expectations regarding technical proficiency, professionalism, morality, and every other facet of leadership must be established and reinforced.

If a SEAL leader cannot master diving, then he cannot lead underwater commando operations. If his professional conduct does not adhere to the values and culture that the SEAL organization promotes, then an example must be made of him in order to deter similar behavior by others. Without accountability, leaders can perform their missions using any method and following any code of conduct. Without accountability, leaders inevitably become irresponsible, lawless cowboys.

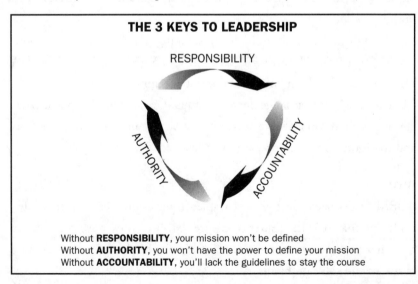

THE 3 KEYS TO LEADERSHIP

RESPONSIBILITY

AUTHORITY

ACCOUNTABILITY

Without **RESPONSIBILITY**, your mission won't be defined
Without **AUTHORITY**, you won't have the power to define your mission
Without **ACCOUNTABILITY**, you'll lack the guidelines to stay the course

LESSON 16
INCREASE YOUR NUMBER OF
LEADERSHIP VEHICLES

THE MISSION

I once led a mission to blow up a ship. I had to know how to launch a mini-sub from a boomer, guide the sub into a harbor, identify the target vessel, plant the limpet mine, and find our way back out to our extraction point. And I had to communicate new directions and ad hoc solutions to my mini-sub pilot while we were underwater, unable to understand each other though the flooded communications devices, and in the dark for hours. Those two leadership skills—technical knowledge and the ability to communicate—were the chief requirements for running that operation. My title as mission commander established the basis from which to leverage these other leadership vehicles, but by itself it had little bearing.

Other SEAL operations emphasized different leadership vehicles. All required some of the vehicles listed below, however, although in different amounts. A SEAL leader will be lost if he can't muster all of them when he needs to.

THE TAKE-AWAY

Having rank and position is useful. Knowing someone important and influential is definitely handy. But if name dropping and waving your rank around are the only ways you can lead, then you're a failure.

Technical Leadership

Do you know what you're talking about? Jon has led many diving missions. His chief and leading petty officer (both expert jump masters) led parachute operations. An expert rope master led rappelling operations. If Jon wasn't the expert in a certain operation, and most of the time he wasn't, he ceded control to whoever was the expert, while retaining veto power. But that worked only if Jon had sufficient technical knowledge to know when to veto a procedure. He never touched the platoon experts who had bathed in the material for years, but it was critical that he was up to speed on every operation they conducted. If he wasn't, he'd just be a rubber stamp for whatever they wanted to do.

Organizational Leadership

Can you manage? One of Jon's jobs as a SEAL platoon commander was to create a capable commando organization that could operate with or without him. Doing this meant establishing a strong organizational structure that emphasized individual decision-making authority at the lower levels, and yet emphasized fast and effective communication up and down the ladder. If Jon had given a sniper team the authority to make a shot, he wanted that team to be able to make the shot, and to inform him quickly. When jumping, he wanted his air department head to do what was necessary to ensure that the jump equipment was ready, and to be able to push issues upstairs quickly if necessary.

Leading also means being able to continually rebuild the structure in order to ensure a customized organization for each operation. Conducting a raid on an enemy camp in the jungle required first two squad-sized forces to assault the camp; then multiple small teams to conduct security, search for intelligence, and set explosive charges; and finally one large team as the platoon left the area. Throughout that mission, the engaged platoon quickly assumed a series of different structures. In each temporary structure, platoon members assumed a series of different jobs, including, at times, what had been their peers' or their bosses' jobs. And the entire time, they operated within a chain of command and in accordance with the overall mission.

Knowledge Leadership

Can you deliver the bigger picture? During a campaign in the Middle East, a task unit Jon led was faced with a choice between two unpleasant staging locations. Both had awful temperatures. However, one consistently offered short showers (although the shower water was 120°, forcing you to stand to one side and collect hot water in your hands, then toss it over yourself after it had cooled a little). The other did not have any reliable shower facility. However, the location without reliable showers had a variety of food from a local village (although this often took the form of suspect meat, outdated dairy products, and tainted vegetables). Dealing with the local officials in the country with sometimes-tainted meat was easier than dealing with the local officials in the country with consistent showers. But the country with local officials who were easier to deal with was also farther from the headquarters component, which meant fewer communications with Jon's bosses. (Of course, that was seen as both bad and good.)

While the platoon was wrestling with the relative lack of merits of the two countries, it was good to inject the perspective and intentions of the higher commands—what was being planned and what missions were in the works. As it turned out, an operation was being considered for which it would be advantageous to be located in the country that had more agreeable local officials, sometimes-tainted food, and unreliable showers.

Inspirational Leadership

Can you persuade people to move mountains, day after day? There will come a time when the facts, expert opinions, and weather do not favor you. This happened to Jon once when he was working with one of the most capable, experienced, deserving platoons in the Middle East. It had been selected for deployment to Afghanistan. Then, shortly before the deployment, orders came down that the platoon had been selected to stand by for what was, at best, a slim possibility of a suspect mission somewhere else. This meant that the platoon would sit out in the sand for 6 months, out of the way, without any hope of directly operating against the primary culprits of September 11.

The platoon had to be informed of the new situation, of course, and given their new marching orders. But ensuring that the members continued to be motivated and fired up, which is much of what it takes to be capable, amounted to what was referred to as "a real leadership challenge."

In this case, the platoon commander had already created a platoon of real professionals and true believers, which made the job a little easier. And the platoon commander took the news soberly. Even so, it was a tough sell when the platoon commander laid it on the line to his men. He didn't hide the facts or pretend he wasn't disappointed. He spoke honestly about the greater war on terrorism, and about the necessity of staging a platoon for this new potential mission. In the end, he was able to bring the SEAL organization a capable platoon for another few months, when it might easily have withered away.

Moral Leadership

Do your subordinates believe in you? Forget instant cults of personality. Building a solid basis of trust takes a long time, but it's essential if the team is going to automatically go the extra mile. After all, if the team members don't trust you, why should they put out on their own? It's not like SEALs are being overpaid.

Officers simply don't make it through BUD/S unless the enlisted students believe in them. There are too many administrative tasks, physical demands, and emotional burdens. It's simply not possible for anyone to make it through unless the rest of the class puts out for that person. Similarly, it's simply not possible to successfully conduct a commando operation unless everyone involved puts out. There are too many rounds to load, too many contingencies to plan for, and too much gear to get ready to accomplish in an 8-hour day, and the pack could effectively stop working for you after what it considered a reasonable shift.

One night, when Jon was his BUD/S class leader, he stayed up late signing dive sheets and reorganizing the boat crews. The next day, the instructors tore into the team, leading them on a long physical training session and a long, fast beach run. Several miles into it, his legs began to slow. There was nothing he could do. He was simply running out of gas. Jon tried willing his limbs to go faster. He ran with his hands on his shorts, pulling his legs forward. But nothing worked and, to his horror, he began to fade from the pack. The instructors running beside the team saw the blood draining from his face and began to close in. Then Jon felt a hand from a classmate on his back, shoving him forward. And then another. "Goddamn it, Mr. Cannon. We will beat you if you don't keep up." And then he was shoved across the finish line.

Creating trust isn't about popularity contests. It's about never lying to your guys. Not just not lying to them about the risks during the ship attack mission, or about the fact that they'll be living in a crowded slum for the next month, or about the fact that their trip to Thailand afterward has just been cancelled. It means not lying to them about their chances for advancement. It means not waiting for the annual counseling session before you tell a guy that he screwed up on the range. It means telling them right away that an exhausting, thankless job needs to get done. It means that when you say you'll go battle the skipper or get them out of dodge, you really will.

SEAL team commanders have repeatedly, consciously sacrificed their careers to do what was right. They've set unpopular but wise courses, gotten rid of incompetent but well-connected subordinates, and taken public floggings from grandstanding politicians. *"I'm through,"* one skipper said. *"I'm at the end of my rope. I've made too many enemies. But the teams are strong, so keep on charging."*

To the thundering herd, these leaders spoke the gospel and were on their side, and, as a result, the pack knew that it had a life jacket and would stay afloat. The most meaningful phrase a leader can ever hear is, *"I believe in you, sir."*

LESSON 17
ASSIGN AN HONEST BROKER
TO BRING YOU BACK TO EARTH

THE MISSION

SEAL team commanders have command master chiefs. Platoon commanders have platoon chiefs. One of a chief's primary roles is simply to tell the boss how it really is. Morale is low? The chief will say so. Your plan falls short? The chief will tell you.

I was once giving our commander a mission briefing on a limpet attack operation when the skipper suddenly asked me what the keel depth of the target vessel was. This was rudimentary stuff, but in the rush to prepare the briefing, my intelligence reps had simply not gotten that information. I told the skipper that since we were attacking the vessel at a shallow depth, it didn't matter what the keel depth was. The skipper nodded and then said he was taking a 5-minute break. As soon as he left, my chief pulled me aside and said, "Don't try to snowball the skipper. You look bad, and it won't work." The chief already had the intelligence reps pulling the right data out. When the skipper returned a few minutes later, the keel depth was written on the briefing board, like the skipper knew it would be.

THE TAKE-AWAY

The more authority you assume, the more you need someone who is assigned to tell you the truth. This is because the more important you become, the more others are apt to tell you what you want to hear. *"Yes, sir. Cinderblocks.com sounds like a real money maker." "No, sir. Everyone completely understands why slashing their paychecks by 10 percent is completely unrelated to your new BMW purchase."* Do these examples really sound far-fetched? They shouldn't.

When you were further down in the ranks, how often did you see a bad idea or lousy prototype take off simply because no one had the guts to disagree with upper management? Guess what? Nothing's changed since you've been promoted. Bad ideas are still being put on your desk. And some of your ideas stink, but everyone's afraid to say so.

Find a tough soul who will stick it to you. Tell him he is your monitor on how things are going. Meet with him regularly. Train him to give you bad news by thanking him for doing so. Talk about everything. You may not agree. You may not take action. But listen to what he has to say.

LESSON 18
THEN SEEK OUT AND LISTEN TO THE REST OF YOUR PEOPLE

THE MISSION

The majority of your good ideas will come from your people, not you. There are more of them, and they are closer to the problems on the ground.

We were in the Western Pacific, on patrol toward a simulated enemy camp that we were to destroy, when we had to hide in the bush. The area turned out to be patrolled frequently. Even though we were, by that time, close to our objective, the bush was filled with thick growth, and travel through it had been slow. Now we couldn't move at all, and we were running out of time. At the same time, leaving the bush meant crossing several well-traveled roads on which we would be exposed. Meanwhile, we had to hit the target right after sunset in order to get far enough out to sea to reach our extraction ship in time. That meant traveling toward our target in daylight.

I gathered my team around. They all crawled up. I went around, asking each person for ideas. In the end, I used several ideas from a few of them, consulted with the chief and my leading petty officer, and announced the new plan. It included their idea of having an advance squad cross a wide field and take up positions at an intersection while the rest of us crossed one of the feeder roads. It included the idea of sending out a squad to ambush any enemy vehicles on the roads immediately before we departed, allowing us to sprint back to the beach instead of patrolling cautiously.

THE TAKE-AWAY

A consultant we know once worked for a company where progress on a project had slowed down to a crawl. Lots of time had been spent analyzing the market and developing strategy but no one could determine the problem. The consultant interviewed the CEO, who seemed sincere and enthusiastic. When he left the CEO's office, he rode the elevator down with one of the programmers, who asked him whom he had seen. The consultant admitted that he had just spoken with the CEO. "Really?" the programmer said, clearly amazed. "It's been more than a year since he's come down and talked with us."

It's essential that your employees know that you are interested in what they have to say. Are you going to make your budgets this year? Are your team members dissatisfied and looking for other jobs? Is the computer system you're relying on benefiting your department or holding it back? Are your clients satisfied or getting ready to leave? Tell them to push it up through their chains of command, but tell them that you're listening. If people conclude they mean little to you, problems are going to arise. First, your people are going to feel disenfranchised and that prevents work from getting done. *Why should I care?* Second, you're going to have an incomplete picture of what's going on. *I had no idea everyone had to work overtime because so many other people had quit.* Finally, you'll miss out on a chance to test your lines of communication. *Jill, I just found out that our inventory levels are way out of bounds. Why didn't you let me know?*

Create conduits that allow your staff to give you feedback and information. Seek out their ideas and concerns on projects. They know far better than you do about what's going on in the trenches. Or stay in your pen until after dark, and then go out and step on that land mine that everyone else knew was there.

LESSON 19
BE UNAPOLOGETIC WHEN YOU FIRE SOMEONE

THE MISSION

Firing someone is possibly the toughest thing you'll ever have to do, but if you can't do it, then you'll never get complete accountability from your people. Your refusal to thin the ranks will be correctly assumed to be your acceptance of deadwood. Your inability to tell people that they have to leave will be correctly seen as giving what is good for an individual priority over what is good for the team.

This is not about having to fire the rude, unpopular, incompetent, unapologetic thief in your organization. If you can't even do that, then return this book. There is no hope for you. This is about having to fire the nice guy whom everyone likes, but who isn't, and who never will be, right for the job. This is about being the unfair, heartless guy.

There was a nice guy in the SEAL organization whom I thought of as a friend. He was in the same training course during an early part of my commando career. He was fairly intelligent, he was fit, and he had good intentions. Unfortunately, he couldn't operate. He wasn't a very good shot. He was a complete mess underwater. He didn't have an aggressive streak that compensated for his lack of aptitude. In fact, he was overly nervous about taking risks, and his nervousness affected his ability to remember basic procedures. He was seen as a safety risk. Everyone liked him, but no one wanted to be his swim buddy.

The class tried to help him out. I talked with him. He was a good guy who deserved help. But in the end, I stopped helping him. I still think of him as my friend and as a good guy, and I don't feel good about having him separated from the SEAL organization. But he wasn't in the right line of work. He was told that without apology. He was forced to go find another job, hopefully one that he was more suited for. I feel bad but it was the right decision. There are a lot of worse feelings when someone dies in training or during an operation because of ineptitude.

THE TAKE-AWAY

Firing someone isn't a decision you make on the fly. It's not an emotional act that you haven't thought through. If it is, then you may face the embarrassing realization that you just fired the main guy your clients trusted or the only woman who knew about Hispanic marketing. And it'll be even worse when you have to explain to your boss that you endangered the company because you didn't know what you were doing when you fired the worker.

But since you're not firing someone for the wrong reasons, and because firing them will help your organization, you have nothing to be embarrassed about. So don't apologize. That only communicates that you're doing something wrong. Yes, it's a difficult decision, probably one of the most difficult ones you're going to have to make. And it's definitely more difficult for the person you just canned. But it's not wrong. It's a business decision, not a personal one—or at least it had better be.

Explain why it was made. Explain that it wasn't a decision you enjoyed making. Keep in mind that it was necessary for the team. Don't change you mind when you see the person cleaning out his or her desk.

LESSON 20
ENFORCE YOUR CHAINS OF COMMAND

THE MISSION

I have a question about my travel orders. So I'll go right to the four-star Commander of all Special Operations. Never mind whatever operation or political issue he's concerned with during his 18-hour day. This is important. Besides, I know he can do something to get me out of that indirect flight through Baltimore. Why shouldn't I go directly to the top with this issue? Because if I do, I'll be professionally but directly pointed back downstairs where someone more appropriate can deal with my question.

Once, when my platoon was deployed in the Western Pacific, we were based at a small forward SEAL operating base. I was a lieutenant at the time, and my platoon members ranged from junior enlisted men and young officers with 2 years in the teams to a seasoned chief who had been everywhere at least twice.

The skipper of the compound had just given a briefing and I was leaving his office when one of my junior platoon members caught up with me. "Mr. Cannon, can I take the truck out to town today to pick up supplies?"

I didn't care whether or not he used the truck. He was capable enough to make his own decisions on how to secure supplies. But he had come to me. I had obviously failed in maintaining the system.

"Have you gone to your leading petty officer?" I asked him.

"No," he replied.

"Have you talked with the chief?"

"No."

"Well you need to go to them first." I then repeated what I had said when we first formed up as a platoon. "My door is always open. You can always come and see me. But you have to use the chain of command. You first go to your immediate boss, and then to his boss. At the very least, you have to let them know that you're coming to see me."

After he turned away, I went and found my chief. "What kind of system are you encouraging when one of your men comes directly to see me without going through his boss first?" I asked. "Don't you have control over your men?" My chief simply nodded in agreement and told me not to worry. After I left, he went to the leading petty officer and, I'm sure, said pretty much the same thing that I had. The fire quickly worked its way down to the junior platoon member's direct boss.

Communication works fast in the platoon. Information moves quickly both up and down the ranks. The chief and petty officers work hard to make sure that issues are resolved right away, and they also know that most of these problems can be taken care of without going directly to the top. If too many people are given immediate access to the top, at all times and for all issues, you'll soon find yourself swamped and your ability to lead severely compromised. You'll become a technician of sorts, handing out permissions, directing traffic, dealing with everything on an inefficient micro level. And the thing is, everyone will immediately go to the top if they are encouraged to do so. After all, why go to your immediate boss when you can circumvent him or her and enjoy the air conditioning further upstairs?

THE TAKE-AWAY

Talk is cheap. People complain about how much junk email they get and how the open-door policy brings a continuous stream of visitors to their offices. But how often do they do anything about it? We're not referring to the everyday questions and opportunities to shoot the breeze. These should be answered with a smile.

No, We're talking about issues that have no bearing on your job. These are issues that directly affect your productivity. How many hours do they sap from your workday? Too many is the answer. So the question isn't where to draw the line on what's important. The question is, "What can be done about it?" How do you direct someone away from you so that you can tackle the tasks at hand?

Often we don't act because we are afraid that we'll be seen as being rude. *"If I let him know that I've actually been off the repackaging project for 8 months, he might think I'm not interested."* Maybe, but more likely he'll simply delete your name from the project. Or we are afraid we'll be seen as avoiding work. *"If I honestly tell him that Wendy is more competent in this field, Wendy will think I'm passing my work off on to her."* Maybe, but it's the right thing to do if Wendy can provide the correct answer and you can't. Or we're afraid that by telling our subordinates' subordinates not to copy us on everything, we'll be out of the loop. *"If I tell Ben to only email his boss, Ken, on this, I'll have to depend on Ken to pass it along."* Maybe, but if you can't depend on Ken, you have a bigger problem on hand.

Think this way: Your team members are, by birth, independent, potentially wild individuals whose behavior is largely constrained by the guidelines and fences you actively maintain. Sorry, but it's true. You need to help teach the guidelines or the others will continue to forage and hunt where the pickings are best. Furthermore, by not enforcing the rules, you are allowing the slow disintegration of your chain of command, and the gradual destruction of your organization.

Do this: The next time you receive repeated emails that have nothing to do with your work or interest, email back the following: *"Dear so and so, thanks for the email but this doesn't concern me. I don't work on this project. I appreciate the heads up, but please take my name off your mailing list on this matter. Thank you."*

The next time someone comes to your office, sincerely find out if you are the best one to help. If you are the best person to help, do so. If you aren't, point the person in the right direction. *"I'm not familiar with this. Let me point you to someone who can help you better."* If it's obvious that the person should have initially started several levels down, make that clear. *"Have you checked with Bob? You should before coming up here. Let me point the way."* And if it's clear that the person has needlessly gone around his or her boss to come to you, educate the individual well. *"You need to go through your boss first. By going around her, you're keeping her out of the loop. Do you understand that?"*

Then call his or her boss and ask why his or her people are coming directly to you.

LESSON 21
DON'T MAKE WORK
YOUR EMPLOYEES' LIFE

THE MISSION

One afternoon when I was working in Eastern Europe, a Special Forces buddy pulled up in his vehicle to take me to work. "We're going to talk to the colonel today," he said, referring to the head of a police battalion in a neighboring district. We drove along the crumbling roads until we pulled into the small, isolated compound in the farm country, with black uniformed guards in front.

Inside, we shook hands with the colonel's aide and were shown into the colonel's office, where we shook hands again and sat down. Two men entered and stood behind us, which I thought was unusual. My buddy began the conversation with a review of the proposed time line for inspecting and collecting some of the colonel's weapons. But the colonel turned the conversation to our health and our local interests. Soon, we were chatting about the town's sports team and joking about foreign television programming. The colonel lit up a cigarette and offered his pack to us, which we turned down. Then the colonel mentioned that a suspected war criminal we had recently apprehended was a close friend of his family's. He became quiet and studied us. I was aware of the men in cheap civilian suits moving closer behind us.

The colonel reached down and slid open a desk drawer out of sight. I eased my hand down to my weapon. There was no sound from my buddy's direction. Then the colonel was sitting upright again, and BANG! It wasn't the gun we feared but a bottle of Johnnie Walker. "But that's not your problem," the colonel said. "First we drink. Then we talk."

THE TAKE-AWAY

There is a manager we know who tells his subordinates, seriously, "If I repeatedly find you in here late at night, I'm going to assume that either I'm giving you too much work or you're not competent enough to do the work I give you."

There are some industries in which there is no way around working late. And the employees who fight for those jobs are fully aware of this when they do so. Other jobs include a period of indoctrination that involves long hours and tough assignments. It makes people part of the club. If that's part of your business, here's to you.

But there's a difference between working late and working to death. Make your employees go home, go to the ball game, or go fishing. Remind them there's a whole world out there. They'll be awake, productive, and involved when they're around. And it will give them a world of experience to bring to the job.

LESSON 22
THERE IS A FINE LINE BETWEEN TRADITION AND OBSOLESCENCE

THE MISSION

The greatest helicopter pilot I have ever known was a woman who lived next to us in Panama and who flew in and out of the jungle to resupply us in the upper Amazon. We camped out on mountain peaks and in deep valleys. Often she arrived during awful weather, having flown for hours through torrential rain to land in strong winds on the side of a muddy, crumbling cliff with half of one tire over the side.

If she could spare an hour, she would get out and stretch and play poker with us. More often than not, though, she was able to get the boxes and parcels out onto the drenched landing zone and then roar off again. If we called for evacuation, she'd haul our asses out of there.

Eventually, however, regional newspapers heard about her, and caricatures of her appeared in the editorial sections. There would be a picture of a voluptuous woman in high heels and lipstick flying a toy helicopter: "La Pilota." Some of the locals smiled. *What's the problem?* She was strong and shrugged it off.

Then our camp became known, and she was ordered to fly several reporters in to our location so that they could report on the war. She did as she was ordered and flew at treetop level, up and over the peaks and down into the steep valleys. Soon the reporters crammed in back were vomiting into their suit pockets. Yes, the image portraying her was part of the camp's tradition by that time. But she never let anyone forget that she was still one hell of a pilot who was never going to lose her edge.

THE TAKE-AWAY

Traditions can strengthen or damage a company. Some of them promote an atmosphere and harmony that raises cannot buy. Others, while ancient, serve no current value other than to damage team integrity. *But we've always given Nancy a hard time about her dress. But workers have always used manual typewriters. But we've always given across-the-board raises despite their individual achievements.*

SEALs give each other a hard time. The biggest charley horse Jon ever got was on the day on the day his skipper pinned a Trident on his chest. Instructors rode him hard to make him learn. Taught him why he needed to be with his buddy at all times. They took a mob and fine-tuned it into a tightly knit group. Although it didn't seem like it at the time, that taskmaster made them pay in training so that they put on their lifejackets the next time, so that they lived. Pain wasn't the objective. It was the vehicle for enlightenment.

Similarly, the team that jokingly writes "The top 10 reasons why Rob/Sue/John went to finance" isn't necessarily trying to hurt someone. It's fun. It raises morale. The company that maintains its original building isn't necessarily unconcerned with working conditions. It's upholding the traditions and culture that define its values.

What purpose does a tradition at your company serve? Morale? Teamwork? Pride? In the end, all of these have a direct influence on productivity. Likewise, what damage is your tradition causing? Lost workdays? Low productivity? Add up the plusses and minuses. Then keep the traditions or get rid of them fast.

LESSON 23
LET THEM BE ANGRY
WHEN THEY HAVE A RIGHT TO BE

THE MISSION

Early in one deployment to the Middle East, we were shelled repeatedly. The first time it happened, we had little warning. Most of us were still working when the first explosion went off and a big fireball erupted to the east. It was terrifying and exciting. And then it was over. We all told each other that we'd have a big party when this was all over.

Two weeks later, we huddled in the tiny, makeshift bomb shelter that we had built. It was constructed out of sandbags with metal plates laid on top. You had to crawl inside and sit with your knees up against your chest and your head crooked forward. Everyone pressed against one another because it was just barely large enough to hold all of us. Sometimes we would sit like that for hours.

And the SCUDs would be inbound. The land would rock and shake when they went off. Then someone would say, "That was closer than last time" and we'd all go off on him. Then the ground would shake again, and we'd get it even worse.

When this happened, no one tried to convince us that everything was all right, or that everything would get better. We weren't dumb. If anything, the bosses shared our sentiments. Then, a few weeks later, we moved to a different location and what had happened didn't matter anymore.

THE TAKE-AWAY

If you're not going to give your workers a raise, you have your reasons. But don't expect them to be happy. Explain the facts to them. Profits tanked last year. *We had a choice between doing this and laying you off.* They may understand, but they don't have to like it. But in the end, if they're not disappointed, they're not human.

When this happens, let them know that you're not happy with the situation either. You'd love to be able to give them a raise. You'd also love it if they got to work early or stopped calling in sick so often. You'd love to have the economy be better. You'd love to have more customers buying your products. Don't fake it. They won't believe you. Get their sentiments out in the open then and there. Then you can respond. Then it will be closer to becoming a thing of the past: "We already spoke about that."

LESSON 24
TELL THEM WHEN THE SHIP IS SINKING

THE MISSION

One evening while we were operating in the Middle East, we were quickly summoned to the skipper's hut where we were told that our small forward base was about to be overrun. The commanding officer calmly but directly told us our situation. A column of enemy tanks had broken through and was speeding toward our position. In a few minutes, they would be upon us. We would not have the weapons or numbers to defeat them.

A brief moment of digestion followed, the skipper laid out his plans, and the platoons immediately fell into their respective missions. Some squads began the emergency destruction of classified equipment and documents. Others readied vehicles and provisions for an escape. Still others formed a line on one side of the base, to stall the advancing enemy tanks and buy a few more moments for the other squads.

There was no time for depression or hysteria. Our missions were clear and imperative. Through their completion, we could prevent a tactical defeat from turning into a rout. Codes and special weapons would not fall into enemy hands. Some of us would survive to fight another day. The skipper's brief meeting was so forthright and compelling that we all enthusiastically fell in for the fight. There was even lighthearted banter when the executive officer outlined our escape and evasion plan. Those of us on the forward line lay prone with adrenaline at full bore as we waited for the first sign of the enemy.

THE TAKE-AWAY

To reduce your losses, bring every available asset into the fight. When the *USS Stennis* rehearses battle drills, every person on the ship—several thousand crew members—is awake and doing something to defend the ship or fight back. Crew members launch planes, employ fire-control radar, coordinate defenses, and plan counterattacks. They are decked out in fire-fighting gear, handling stretchers, standing beside operating tables, closing air locks, operating pumps, and readying construction materials to hold back the sudden, violent onrush of seawater following the explosion of an inbound missile.

When news of an incoming missile is broadcast over the intercom, there is no chaotic rush to the lifeboats.

Instead, the crew understands that it can still win the battle even if the ship begins to lose freeboard. The ship can be leveled. Jets can still be launched. The crew can still accomplish its mission. The ship's descent can be arrested. Crew members know their best chance of survival depends on their not immediately rushing for the lifeboats but remaining at their battle stations.

Even if the unthinkable occurs and the *Stennis* eventually does go down, the ship will be abandoned in a manner that ensures the maximum number of survivors. The skipper and senior master chief will not quietly shimmy over the side during the catastrophe and escape in a lifeboat, leaving the uninformed crew behind.

Similarly, companies can confront issues by informing their workforces of the risks that lie ahead and of the possible consequences. Workers tend to work harder when their livelihood is threatened. Managers tend to manage more effectively. An involved, educated workforce is more likely to help stabilize an organization descending into the depths.

If the organization continues to settle into the water, an informed workforce is more likely to understand the steps that may be necessary—reorganization, longer hours, pay cuts, and lost jobs—to arrest its decline. If the company is lost, an informed workforce will have had the opportunity to seek employment elsewhere, adjust household budgets, and reallocate pension plans.

On the other hand, if your company suddenly goes down in the middle of the night because you chose not to tell your employees about the gaping hole in the side, then you wasted your best opportunity to right your situation. If, during the final moments, you prioritized the size of your golden parachute over the well-being of your workers who are still concentrating on their jobs, then you are similar to a ship's captain who takes the first seat in the lifeboat while the crew is still bailing. And if your ship is in this mess to begin with because you secretly sold off the nautical charts, cancelled your disaster insurance, fired your iceberg watch, or falsified the crew's bounty in the hold, all so that you could finance that luxurious third home, then you should be made to walk the plank. You will have hurt, if not destroyed, many innocent and hard-working people. You were never a leader. You just happened to find a way to get paid the most.

LESSON 25
COMMUNICATING HYSTERIA WON'T DRIVE PRODUCTION

THE MISSION

Once, while we were training to take down an enemy base, I needlessly was a pain in the ass to just about everyone else in my platoon. Our mission was to make our way through heavy jungle to the enemy camp, assault the facility, and destroy several pieces of sensitive equipment through the use of several high explosive charges. Our secondary objective was to collect intelligence while we were inside the camp.

The operation required that the platoon move upriver on boats to a secure drop-off point, patrol through the jungle toward the camp, assault the camp using two squads, and then operate within the camp, in several smaller elements. Accordingly, the platoon was organized into squads that could further be broken down into a security team, a demolition team, a command and control team, and an intelligence team.

Almost immediately upon being dropped off, we began to fall behind schedule. The patrol through the jungle took longer than we had expected. We were not given a GPS during this training event, and we moved by compass and pace counts. The thick brush frequently caused us to weave and bend. Cutting through the brush slowed our speed considerably. There were no mountain peaks or terrain features from which to take a compass bearing. Thick canopy and a cloudy night sky ensured that we made our way in almost pitch-black conditions. By the time we stumbled to within eyesight of the enemy camp, we were still within our window but hours behind our optimal timeline.

The assault went without a hitch. My assistant led the crossfire, and we moved through the compound quickly. Within the camp, I ran the command and control team. That meant that after sending the security, intelligence, and demolition teams out, all I had to do was wait and keep track of the time while they did their jobs, and then direct the exit from the camp and patrol back to our extraction point. Everyone was expertly trained and clearly understood their jobs. Within a few minutes, we would be out of there.

Nonetheless, I was suddenly hit by a bad case of the jumps shortly after sending the various teams out. The demolition team was made up of several demolition elements, each simultaneously handling a different target. One of the fuses on one of the charges came undone and had to be replaced. I began yelling at the element commander to get the bleeping thing done right. My leading petty officer, who ran the demolition team, hurried over from his own element to oversee the procedure. I reminded him that his team was behind schedule, every 10 seconds. "We're at 30 seconds!" I screamed. "Let's go! We're now at 40 seconds!" After one of my outbursts, my leading petty officer paused and collected his thoughts, a 2-second delay that sent me off again. "We need to go now!" I screamed.

Then it was done. The fuses were in place and ignited. I jerked the demolition and intelligence teams in and led us out. The security team fell in behind us. During the patrol out, I had several hours to consider my bout of idiocy.

Afterward, during the postmission briefing, one of the instructors confirmed what everyone in the platoon already knew. "Sir," he pointed out, "you weren't helping anyone move faster there in the compound." During the 55 seconds we had been in the camp, I had been the equivalent of a casualty. I had simply howled and slowed everyone else down.

THE TAKE-AWAY

As a leader, do you stand over someone's shoulder as they hurriedly work on a paper for you? Do you tap your fingers on the table where your programmer is trying to jam out another 100 lines?

If this describes you, realize that you're working against your goal of receiving a quality product on time. In fact, you're screwing it up worse. Do you see the way they sit uncomfortably in front of you, *as if someone were watching them from behind?* That's because they are reacting to you. They are grimacing as a result of your bellows. Those quick nods are in response to your scattered directions. They are only muttering incomplete replies to your questions because they are trying to focus on your goddamn precious project.

When you do this to a subordinate, pause and ask yourself the following:

- Are you acting this way not so much because the project needs to get done soon—which it does—but really because you're angry with the lack of motivation in your subordinate when it's obvious that this is the most urgent task ever assigned in the company?

- Are you acting this way because you are about to be micromanaged, yourself, by your boss because this project was due upstairs a week ago?

- Are you acting this way because you need to walk your subordinate through every step of the way, because your subordinate is too stupid to do it unaided?

If any of these are true, back off. Your impatience, fear, or anger is too late to help. It would have been better if you had properly trained and motivated your workforce ahead of time. It would have helped if you had better managed the project so that you weren't working at the eleventh hour. It would have been better if you had prepared for emergencies such as this beforehand. If you had prepared yourself!

Oh, well. That's all spilled milk, now. Now your priority is to maximize the workers you have on hand, who are at the training and motivation levels you have allowed to exist. Take a breath. Count to 10. Determine a realistic finish time. Force yourself to leave the room. Communicate reality to your boss. Let your people work. Afterward, when the project is complete, you can clear out the dead wood.

LESSON 26
COMMUNICATE THAT YOU TRUST THEM

THE MISSION

There is a story circulating in the Navy about a destroyer whose skipper ordered the lower decks to be repainted gray. A petty officer was assigned the task, he collected his mates, and soon the job was completed. Since the color of the new gray paint was the same as the old gray paint, it was difficult in the low light to tell if new paint had been applied, so the crew members hung "wet paint" signs everywhere.

When the petty officer reported to his division officer that he had completed his task, the division officer came down and looked over the work that looked satisfactory. Then, despite the posted signs, the division officer dipped his finger against a bulkhead, coming away with a great smear of gray paint on his fingertip.

The division officer reported to his department head that the painting had been completed. The department head also descended below decks to inspect the work, and also tested the gray paint with his finger. The department head told the executive officer, who did the same thing. That evening, there was an all-hands meeting on board during which all the officers stood to one side. The crew looked at the officers. Every one of the officers' forefingers, including the skipper's, was covered with gray paint. Whatever was verbally put out during the meeting has been forgotten. What was communicated to all the members of the crew was that their officers didn't trust them to do their work.

The strength and core of U.S. commando teams, similar to the U.S. military as a whole, are its ranks of dedicated, noncommissioned professionals. These aren't the officers. These are the chiefs and petty officers in the SEALs and their equivalents in the Special Forces—the technical and operational specialists—who actually accomplish the mission. Petty officers, whose peers back home are working in gas stations, are delivering satellite imagery of the terrorist caves they just destroyed. Few other militaries in the world push decision-making authority down to the enlisted ranks. And that's too bad. Combined with superior training and a solid culture of professionalism, the result is a workforce that rises to the high level of responsibility thrown at it.

To leverage the skills of its workforce, commando officers go to great lengths to understand the skills and capabilities they have on hand. Officers go through the same training as enlisted commandos. They routinely spend time in the armory, dive locker, parachute loft, intel shop, and every other technical department on which they depend. They routinely participate alongside the technical masters in the trade at hand. They know precisely what their men can do.

At the same time, they don't pack static-line parachutes and they don't recalibrate dive sensors. They know enough to trust their men to do so. To insist on doing these tasks would be to communicate that they don't trust their men.

Several years ago, we conducted a training jump near the Coronado Bridge in San Diego. I dangled from a parachute packed by a petty officer. I jumped out an airplane based on the direction of a chief. After I landed in the water, I swam to a rubber boat that had been similarly parachuted down by a petty officer.

I could have been in everyone's hair during the preparation instead of planning the mission. And things probably would have turned out all right if I had stayed within my knowledge. But I might as well have been screaming "I don't trust you!" And if I overstepped my expertise, well, commandos are not shy about calling you on it. There's nothing quite like an officer suddenly stepping in, taking over, and generally messing up what a completely competent petty officer was doing just fine.

THE TAKE-AWAY

Here's a story from a friend who worked in the auto business. A redesign had been ordered for one of the company's great sport cars and the marketing team spent months collecting and analyzing data and developing prototypes. Finally the team had a redesign in mind for delivery. It was gorgeous. It incorporated every piece of consumer information and every production requirement into an amazing and compelling form.

The team brought the vice president in charge down to look at the lifelike, clay model they had built. He looked at it, gouged a big trough of clay to one side with his hand to make a makeshift spoiler, and said, "No, no, no. What are you thinking? It should look like this. . . ." From that point on, he was in their faces every day. He didn't simply redirect the focus of the project—which would have been understandable. Perhaps he knew something they didn't.

Instead, he was down at the lower levels, personally overseeing minor work. Managers who had spent weeks building new concepts were overturned on what seemed like whims. He oversaw minute details. He was the highest paid assistant brand manager in the business. To him, everyone else was obviously incompetent. And the care never went into production.

Don't do this.

Know your people. Know what they do. But understand the difference between knowing your workers' jobs and doing them for them. Nothing will make your workers as proud, loyal, and productive as when they have the knowledge that you believe in them.

LESSON 27
KICKING THEM UNNECESSARILY
REVEALS YOUR INCOMPETENCE

THE MISSION

There needs to be a reason for inflicting pain. When I was in BUD/S, one of the students fell asleep with the radio. That was reason enough. His boat crew had been out in the bush for a while, and they were all exhausted. He was the radioman, and when it was his turn to take a break, he lay down with his mouth right next to the microphone. He fell asleep. And he slept in such a way that the microphone key was depressed. And all across the radio waves—on the other platoons' radios, in the instructors' tent, and in the communications headquarters—one could hear loud, continuous snoring. And there was no way to contact the platoon, because he was asleep with the radio locked in his hand with that one channel already opened. The channel with the loud, continuous snoring.

The next morning, when the instructors located the boat crew, there was hell to pay. The officer had to carry large rocks—"dinosaur eggs"— up and down a steep mountain. And throw himself in the water. And make sugar cookies out of himself in the sand. But the radioman, he had to carry his radio from that point on. This wasn't a cell phone. This was a heavy, shock-resistant, steel and plastic crate that you could signal around the world with. He carried it on his back to bed, and through the 20 chin-ups we had to perform whenever we wanted to eat, and on our runs. BUD/S instructors aren't cruel without a purpose; they do their job so that you learn. Our radio sleeper made it through BUD/S, with a deep appreciation for operating communications gear correctly.

There are always those who kick their dog simply because they were kicked themselves. My platoon occasionally attended training programs not attached directly to the SEAL organization. In one particular case, the chief instructor either didn't know who we were or didn't care. He decided that he needed to immediately put the fear of God into us. On the very first day of training, we gathered in front of the compound and he came out yelling as if we were raw recruits. "Stand up straight! Get in ranks!" I walked up and quietly advised him that he really should simmer down. "Don't worry, son. I know what I'm doing!" I looked at my platoon. They were grinning. "Okay," I shrugged and fell back in with my guys.

Then he was all over us. Screaming to tighten up that line. To get back at attention. The guys were laughing. He was red in the face. "Drop and give me 10 pushups." They didn't stop after 10. "Get up!" They went on to 20. "I said 'get up!'" On to 30. "We love you, instructor so-and-so," the platoon sung out. Forty. Fifty. I thought the instructor was going to blow a gut. His fellow instructors came out to see what was going on. Sixty. Seventy. He was shrieking. "I want to have your baby, instructor so-and-so," our chief bellowed as he continued to push them out.

THE TAKE-AWAY

At a job one of us had the pleasure of working, all new hires had to wake up early and produce a spreadsheet in time for the morning briefing. It was a pain. The network was slow early in the morning because everyone was logging on. Everyone there could have been enjoying breakfast during that time. It was complete drudgery, copying numbers and creating a chart. No decision making or analysis was required.

At the same time, by continuously going through this ritual, we learned the codes attached to each of our products. We learned the cyclical trends of our new product sales and which of our products were front-running earners. In short, there was a reason for us waking up early. We benefited from the chore.

At another company one of us once worked for, our team had to produce a paper for upper management. We had plenty of time built into the schedule. The paper was due on a Friday. We agreed to review it Wednesday, two days prior. Additionally, we agreed to meet on Monday, as a pre-review. It was buttoned up. The Friday beforehand, however, a middle manager new to the team approached a coworker and stated that she wanted the project on her desk by noon on Sunday. "Why?" My coworker had made plans for the weekend. "Because that's when I want it." There was no good reason. Perhaps the new manager thought she was asserting her authority. In any case, word got around. Shortly thereafter, her peers were joking about it openly. *"Whatever you do, don't give me my copy until Monday."* Do you think that spells respect? Think again.

CHAPTER 4

THE THUNDERING HERD

THE WAY IT IS

Let's see if we've got this straight. You excelled in school. Hell, you even got an advanced degree from a great university, and you had a meaningful internship at a big-name company. And during those years, you had one helluva time to boot. You built memories for a lifetime, you developed a network of solid friends, and you picked up skills to help you succeed in the real world.

You believe that, as a result of all that education, you're ready for a top management position. Why? Because you know how good companies operate. You've written endless papers and studies on the subject. You've researched and learned, and better still, you've seen the opportunities that the New Economy brings that the old guys don't even know are there. Hell, you've read about it enough; now it's time for you to put that knowledge to work. You can feel it in your gut: If you can just get the responsibility you deserve, you can lift your company up, increase its profits, and be a star.

Hopefully you can. Women and men, fresh out of school, have arrived at the corporate doorstep and quickly mastered their jobs, and then their bosses' jobs. I once worked for a guy who came right out of an undergraduate program and zoomed on to become the youngest category brand manager in the universe. And he's a great guy.

But here's the reality behind it. The SEAL organization wasn't built on the strength of its senior officers, and neither is your company. The SEAL organization, like the Marine Corps or the Rangers or the Army Special Forces, is built on the strength of its teams. And no one person is going to make or break a team. The team is the team. The team is made up of the people who break down doors and the people who back them up. It's based on the skill of the young SEALs who take the shots. It's based on the experience of the chiefs who have deployed around the world a dozen times, and who have the experience to keep the team together when conditions get rough. It's the expertise of the technicians who repair the mini-submarines, salvage the radios, and fix the pay issues.

Senior leadership rotates through each team occasionally in order to make sure that the overall plan is adhered to. These leaders make sure that the big picture is kept in mind. They point the team in the right direction, but without the team, the leaders are nothing. Let me say it again: *Without the team, the leaders are nothing.*

Okay, so now that you know how important and essential you are to the success of a mission and to the success of your business, it's time to take a closer look at the realities that come with the job. No, these realities aren't all pretty. Many of them are directly related to the fact that while you may be in a position of authority, there's almost always someone higher than you whom you must occasionally defer to. To be honest, the majority of these realities suck. But it's necessary for you to understand what they are, so that when you encounter them, you recognize what they truly represent: opportunities for you to grow and excel.

Understanding these realities is absolutely essential to your development, so never shy away from them. In fact, each time you encounter one and triumph over it, think of it as another credit in your ongoing education, because that's what it is. The greatest leaders have been tripped up by and have ultimately overcome each and every one of these obstacles. The pretenders—the people who have the title, the corner office, or the parking space, but not the fundamental leadership skills—have made a career out of avoiding these realities, but you can bet that sooner or later reality will catch up with them. Their careers will end in a fiery blaze of worthless stock options. Or banishment to a lonely retirement.

Are you still wondering what the thundering herd is? Well, it's not just that mass of people who make up the labor force and report to various bosses. It's the ones who are charging forward in an effort to make a difference. It's the ones who realize that there are things they don't know, and are seeking to learn the intricacies of their jobs so that they can rise above and do more. It's the ones who are seeking to grow and someday lead, themselves

It's the guys and girls who are biding their time, waiting for the right opportunity and looking for ways to build their portfolio of experience so that when that opportunity appears, it will be theirs.

"I want linebackers!" a BUD/S instructor used to declare. "Hundred and fifty pounds, two hundred and fifty pounds—I don't care. I want a guy who will lower his shoulder and suck in all the air from the space he wants to be in."

Still wondering who the thundering herd is?

LESSON 1
REALIZE THAT NOBODY'S FORCING YOU TO BE HERE

THE MISSION

The SEAL instructors who train prospective SEALs don't fire any of their students. They don't have to. The students quit on their own.

During basic SEAL commando training, or BUD/S, students continually slog through tough, nasty conditions that replicate what they might have to endure on actual missions. They spend weeks swimming through cold water. They pack heavy weights across the desert. They conduct detail-intensive operations that require equally intensive planning and preparation. And all the while, they get little sleep and endure the rough attention of several overbearing instructors.

As a result, students quickly discover whether being a SEAL is what they really want. Yes, a lot of students find out that they don't want to be SEALs and leave. This is good for the organization. If it didn't happen, the SEAL organization would have to not only continually motivate its people to climb sheer cliffs and attack nuclear submarines, but motivate them to want to be SEALs in the first place.

It's also good for the remaining SEAL candidates, who would otherwise wonder if their lives were at risk because their teammates weren't totally focused on what they were doing. And it's good for the students who leave, so that they can go on to become bankers or lawyers or insurance adjusters, instead of being forced to swim onto enemy beaches or storm terrorist cells.

To help students make their decision, instructors look for particular aspects of being a commando that a particular student might not be comfortable with. Then they pile it on. You get nervous under stress? Instructors will make it their mission in life to stress you out while you try to focus your front-sight bead on the rifle target hundreds of yards away. *"Focus, Ensign So-and-so! And you'd better not make any safety violations, or I'll have you down in the surf zone taking the water temperature for the next few days! What is taking you so long!"*

You're afraid of sharks during long, lonely swims in the middle of the night? You're going to find yourself taking nothing but long, lonely swims in the middle of the night with your swim buddy, waiting for his head to disappear abruptly as he gets dragged underneath.

And of course, for an organization like the SEALs that lives or dies on the strength of the team, the recruits that the instructors really enjoy tormenting are the ones who are not team players. *"Who's the biggest skate in the class? Come on! Give me one name and you can all come out of the surf zone!"* Instructors will heap on scenarios where you live or die depending on whether your peers help you. An officer in my class had to go throw himself in the water every day and then catch up with the rest of the class. The rest of the class pitied him, but their runs didn't slow down. In fact, they got faster in order to get to the chow hall on time. In the evenings, after a day of torture, he would sit alone, sandy and wet. He didn't know it, but he had already been abandoned. You survive BUD/S in part because you don't quit, but also because your peers don't think you should.

For the recruits who decide that being a commando is not their cup of tea, there's a big brass bell in the corner of the training compound. Students simply have to go over and ring it three times to signal that they're out. Sometimes you can tell ahead of time that someone's going to leave. In the first or second week, it's the Rambo types and quasi-Olympic athletes who discover for the first time what it's really like to hurt. Later on, it's the students who begin to complain about how it all sucks, while the other trainees remain mute and disdainful or tell them to shut up. And sometimes you really can't tell. A student suddenly stands up in the surf zone and wades ashore by himself. In either case, it's over. No one is forced to be a SEAL.

THE TAKE-AWAY

It works the same way in the civilian world. In the late 1980s, Jeff was doing time at one of the major film companies in Los Angeles. The position was in the Domestic Theatrical Marketing Department. It was a nice position, but he didn't like his supervisor and he didn't like the way the department was run. The supervisor didn't care for him too much either. So, he went to human resources and explained the situation. They listened, and they agreed that he had some very valid points. They thought there probably were ways to improve the department. But they also told him that this was the way the director chose to run the group, and that while he was a good employee, nobody was forcing him to work there. He had a choice. And as long as he chose to work for that department, he would have to work the way his supervisor thought best.

That was Jeff's last day there. And in the end, this was absolutely the right thing to do, because it taught him something that helped direct the way he looked at employment from then on.

You need to realize that nobody is forcing you to work for a particular company. As a matter of fact, nobody's forcing you to work at all. If you are working somewhere, you are there voluntarily. If you don't want to be there, you have the right to leave. Time is short. Don't waste anyone's time, especially not your own. Get out and get on with your life. Take the opportunity to leave and build your career the way you want to.

If you do decide to stay, then you have to realize that there is a system in place, and there is a structure that you must work within. Yes, that system can be changed, and, yes, that structure can be improved. But that is a long process; it will not happen overnight. If you think there's enough opportunity for you, great; stay and put the effort into improving the way things work. But if you don't think the company you're working for fits your needs, then it's time to move on.

We can't stress the importance of this enough. Don't stay in a dead-end job hoping that things will change. That's an exercise in futility and frustration, particularly when there are a lot of other people who would probably fit that job very nicely. More important, though, staying in a bad position has the potential to ruin your career.

What, is this a leadership lesson as well? Yes. Many a promising leader has made the mistake of staying in a situation that was wrong for her or him. The person stayed either out of pride, out of fear, or simply because he or she didn't have the imagination to believe that things could be different somewhere else. Big mistake. If you're not totally on board wherever you are, then you won't stay focused, and your team will suffer. Results won't be optimum, and you'll look bad. You will cripple your own development as a leader because you'll be so focused on the outward problems of your situation that you'll overlook the inward issues of your team and your leadership of that team.

LESSON 2
IF YOU'RE NEW,
YOU HAVE TO SHUT UP AND LEARN

THE MISSION

Woe to the new young officer in a platoon who gets it into his head that he knows everything!

Every once in a while you hear a rumor about this. In such-and-such platoon, some idiot just out of school decided that he knew how to operate better than the leading petty officer with five deployments under his belt. Or—God forbid—he thought he knew how things ought to be run better than the platoon chief or the commander. At best, this is the result of naïveté and leads to a healthy bout of wake-up-and-smell-the-coffee abuse by the rest of the platoon. At worst, it may end in an embarrassing one-on-one session with the chief or the platoon commander. And if the kid is *really* arrogant, then even those remedies won't turn down the volume on his ego. With a blind faith in his rank and his right to command, he'll embark on a campaign of intentional disloyalty and subversion that will divide and destroy a platoon. The guy will be labeled a dirtbag for life. But his actions will sink the rest of the team.

To stop things like this from happening, new officers are put into the same squad as the platoon chief. Why? Because the chief has been in for years and has forgotten more commando stuff than the new officer will ever learn. The chief is a highly experienced person and will quickly make sure the young officer knows that without the chief's guidance, he's going to be drowning in the maze of new procedures, technical information, and intimidating responsibilities that come with his job. And if the officer goes over the chief's head to complain, that young officer is going to hear a lot of "I don't care if you outrank him, keep your mouth shut and watch what he does."

In the same way, newly enlisted platoon members are put under the care and feeding of more experienced petty officers. Why? Because every one else in the platoon has already deployed several times. All of them know how to restart the outboard motor when you're still 60 miles from shore. They know the best way to get your 9-mm out and on line when your rifle jams. And they know which bars in Pattiya Beach are lousy.

If you're a new recruit or a new officer, you can spend your first few months trying to convince the veterans that you really are the reincarnation of Otto Skorzeny, David Sterling, or Bull Simons, which will probably result only in your getting the crap beat out of you. Or you can take the time to learn how to survive and how to keep your teammates alive. You're expected to be dumb during this period, so take advantage of that and learn. Everyone knows the opportunity to accidentally kill your buddies through a bad decision will come soon enough. There's no need to rush it.

THE TAKE-AWAY

The reason most CEOs are older is that it takes time to acquire enough experience to lead. It doesn't happen overnight. And trying to jump the gun is the best way to screw up. Did you ever wonder why so many start-ups and dot.coms failed? Did you ever wonder why those that succeeded were the ones where an experienced CEO was brought in?

The companies that had great ideas, great technologies, and boatloads of money, but whose people didn't know the first thing about leading, likely did a nosedive when the going got just slightly tough. The companies that had solid leadership had a better shot at moving forward.

Yes, we all know you're bright and educated, and you have a hundred ideas to contribute. But you don't know everything yet. And if you think you know you can jump in and take charge, then you aren't ready to lead. If you had the experience, you'd know that. But no one's born with it. Even flag officers, CEOs, and line managers take the time to learn how things are done and how things work before handling the controls firmly.

If you somehow interview your way into a position that far exceeds your experience, then find your own platoon chief to help you out fast. Other books usually call this sort of person a mentor but that's not what we are talking about. What matters is what this person can do for you. Congratulations on your new job. Now find out what the hell is going on.

Don't waste time on titles. Look for someone who knows how the company works, and by that we mean how it really works, not how the organization chart lays it out. All that matters is that you trust him or her, and that this person can help you maneuver through the organization. The only thing you're likely to prove by bustling forward is how little you know. You can do a lot more good by first shutting up until you have a clue.

LESSON 3
YOU'RE THE ONE WHO CAN MAKE IT WORK, AND THAT'S OFTEN THANKS ENOUGH

THE MISSION

I once had a mini-submarine pilot who had established himself as one of the premier pilots in the SEALs. He could nail a perfectly straight course no matter what the currents or turbulence. He could make precise cuts and map unerring routes through a harbor. He could hover effortlessly so all you had to do was spring the hatch, reach up and plant a mine, and then speed back out of bad-guy land before any patrols knew you were nearby. And he could do all of this in spite of equipment failure, flooded suits, or incomplete intelligence. He was better at what he did than any of the others were at their respective jobs. He would be the one you could always rely on to get you back to the boomer.

To give a team the greatest chance of mission success, his involvement in any particular mission was more important than my own as mission commander. I could plan the mission, sit next to him as he flew, and help plant the mine. But in the end, none of my planning or assistance could replace his ability to fly level, or his ability to get another 15 minutes from the submarine's batteries when, according to the laws of physics, they should have been dead.

But what made him essential to us was that he realized his own importance and the consequences of his actions. He accepted that he would be under water, in frigid temperatures, more often than anyone else. He accepted that he would be deployed away from home more frequently. He accepted that he would undertake more risks. Recognition in the SEAL organization isn't doled out for free. And the best recognition comes because people know you'll get them back alive. This kind of recognition, when it comes, sticks with you forever.

THE TAKE-AWAY

Work is a two-way street. You've been given a job. You're being paid a salary you've agreed to. You have a lifetime's worth of free office supplies. Congratulations. But now the company depends on you. Now it is your turn to put out, work hard, and learn more so that both you and the company will be more successful than before you started. If you're looking for a pat on the back and a pay raise every time you do something right, well, think again. That takes a lot of time and effort away from what everyone else is doing. Besides, continuously having to tell you "thank you" for doing your job becomes a bore. Is that all you're about, Fred? How about taking some pride in doing your job well?

You've got to learn to look to yourself for approval. You've got to learn to acknowledge a tough assignment as another challenge and another way to prove yourself. After all, being given the opportunity to develop as a leader is its own reward. Not just in the satisfaction of watching your team achieve a hard-won objective, but in the knowledge that you were key in their doing so. Hard work and obstacles you overcome are making you into a more able and valuable leader. If you overlook these benefits—if you seek banners and balloons from your boss every day, then you're going to be labeled as a time drain. *How many times do I have to wind this guy up?* Worse, you'll never feel pride in your accomplishments for their sake alone.

LESSON 4
YOUR VALUE DURING THE BATTLE HAS NOTHING TO DO WITH HOW CLOSE YOU ARE TO THE FRONT

THE MISSION

When I was deployed on the aircraft carrier *USS Stennis,* I was struck by the tremendous respect that the strutting, cocky fighter jocks had for the seemingly lowly supply officers (such as the one I shared a room with seven decks down). The F-18 fighter pilots would scream off the decks toward their unknown bombing targets. A few hours later, somewhere deep in the rough terrain of the enemy's territory, a squad of SEALs would transmit the coordinates of enemy caves up to the pilot as he circled overhead. The fighter pilot then entered the coordinates into the brain of the 2000-pound smart bomb slung under his wing, which he then released and which landed with devastating effect. The media reported extensively on this strategy, and many stories about this sort of mission were published. But I don't think anyone ever heard about the supply officers. To hear it from the news reports, you'd think those fighter jocks built those F-18s themselves, and that the SEAL team just magically teleported itself into position.

The pilots and the SEAL platoon were only the tip of a spear that was honed, maneuvered, and thrust by thousands of others. The SEAL platoon was in position to transmit its data because the platoon had been inserted by a Blackhawk helicopter crew. The aircraft pilot was over the SEAL platoon when it signaled because shortly beforehand, a KC-135 aerial tanker circling nearby had pumped several thousand pounds of jet fuel into the thirsty jet.

Hours earlier and 500 miles away, the F-18 pilot had been able to take off because dozens of young handlers who dodged the suction from jet engines and balanced on the rolling deck at night in 40-knot winds had fueled, armed, and launched his fighter. The Blackhawk that inserted the

SEALs had been launched successfully because security guards, counterintelligence agents, and gas turbine experts worked around the clock at the commando camp where it was based.

Earlier still, intelligence specialists, communicators, and experts in joint Navy–Army–Air Force operations had helped plan and coordinate the missions. The contributions of the Seabees, computer specialists, deck hands, and administrative experts allowed the pilot and the SEAL team to focus entirely on their operation. Trainers, logisticians, purchasers, and maintenance crews had ensured that everyone was well trained, equipped, and deployed. And these behind-the-scenes experts depended in turn on the support of legions of recruiters, detailers, and administrators, as well as on welders, cooks, planners, security guards, and maintenance crews of their own.

Somewhere in this mix, my roommate, the supply officer, busted his chops 18 to 20 hours a day, 7 days a week, keeping thousands of sailors fed, dozens of jets fueled, and dozens of smart bombs available. Every one of the pilots I spoke with knew that.

Do you think a war is fought only on the front line? Think again.

THE TAKE-AWAY

Is it all about the guy who makes that final presentation before the client? Is it all about the actor who sheds that tear as the screen fades to black? Is it only about the programmer who figured out how to solve *The Big Problem* in the code?

Did you ever wonder how really good fund managers make their stock picks? When they visit the companies whose stock they buy, they meet the people working there, and they see who's behind the people whose names are on the masthead and whose pictures always make it to the papers. Why do they do this? Because those are the people whose expertise and hard work lead to the company's success or failure.

There are lots of essential jobs that don't make it to the final credits. But insiders and policy makers know who's important to a company. And it's rarely only the person who gets to wear the cool suit.

Yes, we all want to be that person. And in time some of us will be. But the only way to make that time arrive is to be an essential part of the company and the team. Learn as much as you can, continue developing yourself, so that when the opportunity arrives, you'll be front and center.

LESSON 5
HELP YOUR BOSS AND YOU HELP YOURSELF

THE MISSION

When I was on deployment, I once got an urgent directive to move one of my fast boat detachments from the foreign warship where it was berthed to an American warship several hundred miles away. Getting the detachment to the U.S. warship was critical to stage the mission at hand. Our team would not get the mission if we could not move our boats there quickly enough.

However, there were several serious obstacles to getting my team to our objective. The distance between the vessels was too great to drive the boats there directly and still be able to deploy on time. We could fly the boats in cargo planes, but that would require a rendezvous between a specific kind of cargo plane and the boats at a nearby airfield. And none of *those* kinds of cargo planes were available and in the vicinity. As if all that weren't bad enough, there were limited means for actually getting our fast attack boats aboard the U.S. warship even if we did somehow manage to arrive in time.

My team came up with a number of solutions that would enable us to surmount all of these obstacles. However, the Navy—and this should come as no surprise to anyone who has worked in a large organization—has official instructions that prescribe approved methods of transporting fast attack boats, and many of the solutions we came up with were not included in the Navy's recommendations. That's not to say that the Navy disapproved of our solutions. It was just that our solutions hadn't been tested yet. If we tried them, and if something happened and the boats were damaged, it would be our necks for attempting it. As a result, we wouldn't be able to count on automatic assistance from people who, inevitably, were afraid for their careers. Pushing our solutions through would entail lots of wrangling, frustration, duct tape, and elbow grease.

At the same time, there were many advantages to not accomplishing our objective. My task unit had worked and fought hard and unstintingly for many months in an unfriendly part of the world, while enduring arduous living conditions. They were tired. They could be spending this time relaxing in a nearby friendly country. It wouldn't be difficult for them to get out of this job. Any of the issues mentioned could be used as an excuse not to press forward. *"Sorry, sir, but this isn't included in regulations." "Sorry, sir, but there's just no way to transport the boats."* It wouldn't have hurt them. I would be the one who went on record as the task unit commander who couldn't deliver.

Instead of doing this, the detachment huddled and then went to work with a vengeance. The detachment chief took a few years off his life sweating out a plan. The sled dogs tested load tolerances and new makeshift gear. Not long after being given the task, the detachment commander announced that he could make it happen.

Why did they take the hard road when they didn't have to? Because they love their jobs, and operating, and being part of something great. And they disdain the thought of not being able to do something. These guys are supposed to be the we-can-do-it-anywhere-in-the-world guys. If they got their boats on board the warship, they'd be that much closer to conducting an operation. They'd be the guys who'd found a new way to deliver boats express mail. They wouldn't be the guys who had shrugged and given up and let their boss down. What the hell kind of commando is that?

Yeah, I benefited from their drive. The thing is, that detachment commander and his crew are in my book now, even though that wasn't what motivated them. They're known for what they did by senior leadership in the community. They want a recommendation? They want in on something big? They'll be first in line.

THE TAKE-AWAY

Before we go any further, we can already hear you start to object: "My boss is a self-centered idiot. He's no SEAL. His guys would have drowned him if he had gone to BUD/S. Why should I work hard to help him out?" Why? Because (1) if he doesn't look good, you're going to look worse. And (2) no matter how bad your boss is, you can still probably learn a hell of a lot from him or her. No doubt it's tough to work for someone who doesn't return the favor. We've both done it. But in those cases, we've both grown far above where they've remained.

The CEO's job is to set a direction and to make sure the organization works toward it. From there on down, everyone else's job is to manage different aspects of the CEO's plan. Wherever your boss is in the structure, his or her job is to make sure that his or her portion of the plan is being achieved. And you? Your job is to ensure that your boss is successful and looks good.

So what's in it for you? And what's in it for your people? First, there's the trickle-down effect. The better the company performs, the better your bonus, and the better that company name looks on your résumé. The better you make your boss look, the more likely someone—if not your boss, then someone in the corner office—will be to take notice and recommend you for a promotion. And the better the recommendation is, the better you are. Most important, the better your reputation will be, regardless of how your boss individually feels. The reverse is true as well. Give up and slack off, and you confirm what your boss thinks. Your boss's peers who watch you give up won't have any reason to think otherwise. This is not about who's right or wrong, or who deserves or doesn't deserve your support. The fact is, when you help your boss, regardless of whether he or she morally warrants it, you benefit. When you don't help and your team fails, you fail with it. And your whines afterward of "But he started it . . ." will fall on deaf ears.

LESSON 6
IT'S OKAY; YOU'RE SUPPOSED TO FIGHT WITH YOUR BOSS

THE MISSION

A SEAL platoon commander and his platoon chief have a love-hate relationship. There are many subtle ways to lead, and yet the commander must occasionally act decisively, dictating routes and methods. To achieve success, the platoon chief must loyally support his commander. At the same time, the chief can't help but have his own opinion of how things should be run. He doesn't have the same information that the commander has, but he's looking out for the boys and is much better grounded in what's technically feasible. This ensures that the platoon commander and his chief will eventually butt heads. It's supposed to work that way.

The same thing happens between the platoon commander and his junior officers. I led a submarine-launched mission to reconnoiter a base that housed amphibious assault forces. We came through the surf and worked our way inland. When we came to the base, I decided that we needed to get past the barbed-wire fence perimeter and actually enter the facility. One of my assistants crouched with me away from the others and vehemently disagreed with my decision, arguing that entering the base was unnecessary and could compromise our entire mission. I listened, but I disagreed with him. And over the fence we went. I'm sure that throughout the entire time inside the facility, he was muttering about what an idiot I was. But the mission was a success.

Another day, another issue. It was a Friday afternoon, and my platoon chief went ape on behalf of the guys because I suddenly announced that we would be conducting land warfare training that evening. It was raining. Some of the guys had already changed clothes and had plans for the afternoon and night. But I was looking beyond that afternoon and that evening. And so we trained.

THE TAKE-AWAY

A functioning team is more than just a group of people with a common goal. It's a group of people who can work toward that common goal despite having different opinions about how to reach it. No, not everyone has the same say. No, not everyone's opinion will play a part in the end. The boss makes the final decision and will live or hang by that decision.

Will you agree with every decision? No. If you're a leader yourself, it's inevitable that you will have an opposing view or contrary insight. Will you know everything about why a decision is made? Rarely. Do you want to play a part in the mission or project? Of course. And you want the decision that's about to be made to be the right one, the one that will bring you through with flying colors.

So what do you do?

When you disagree with your boss, let him or her know about your ideas. If you don't, you're screwing the team over. Many doomed projects got off the ground because everyone was too frightened to say "boo." On the other hand, many lives and dollars have been saved because someone was willing to speak out. Who knows? Perhaps you do know something that your boss doesn't. Perhaps that's why he or she hired you.

But if, after you tell your boss your alternative plan, she or he still plunges ahead with their original idea, get on board. He or she has listened. He or she has considered what you had to say. And now he or she *still* wants to climb the sheer cliffs while under fire in order to knock out the enemy guns. In this situation, if the decision is within your boss's authority to make, is supportive of the team's mission, and is consistent with your organization's philosophy, then you have to go along. And do the work to the best of your ability.

Oh yes, something to keep in mind. Believe it or not, you may not know the big picture. Maybe those enemy guns on top of those sheer cliffs threaten the entire allied fleet. Maybe your platoon is the only team that can do it. Maybe you'll come out alive and be a hero. Maybe you won't. But that's a moot point. You joined the organization and its decision-making process. So fight with your boss. You're supposed to. Then do your job.

LESSON 7
COWBOYS AND COGS DON'T HAVE JOB SECURITY—TEAM MEMBERS DO

THE MISSION

If you want special attention from the instructors at BUD/S, do one of these two things:

- *Don't stand out.* Hide in the middle of the pack during a blistering beach run. Don't call attention to yourself when the instructors are looking for a defiant sailor to whoop out a war cry. Don't break your back trying to set a new obstacle course record. I once ran back from chow with the rest of the training unit, the heavy rubber boat bouncing on our shoulders, when one of the instructors suddenly yanked me to one side so violently that we all almost tumbled to the pavement. "I don't know who you are," he said. "If I still don't know who you are next time I see you, I will do something with you to make me remember."

- *Show the instructors that you're way above your peers.* Run way ahead of everyone else while some of your buddies are back puking in the sand. Leave your buddy behind at the last pier piling so that you can come in first on a night swim. When a Navy captain I worked for was going through training, the instructors told his class that they were all going to get tortured unless they went out to the beach, then and there, and ran a 4-mile sand course in less then 30 minutes. It was late in the day, and they were already pretty beat up. They took off, every man fighting to get over the finish line in time. The captain I mentioned thought he was going to die as he lurched over the finish, the first in a long, strung-out line of stragglers. Not everyone finished, and the class was promptly taken out into the sand and tortured. "I said I wanted your class to finish the course in under 30 minutes," the chief instructor said.

On the other hand, if you want to stay around, just do this:

Make sure your team succeeds. Lift your buddy up by the back of his T-shirt after his arms have stopped functioning and the instructors want still more push-ups. Take several hundred-round belts from your heavy gunner's pack and put them in your own. After my captain's class was tortured, the instructors said they'd give the class another chance. Run, right now, another 4-mile sand run in less than 30 minutes. Naturally, everyone was just about dead by then. They huddled, and the young officer simply said that they would run as a group. No one was to break away. To this day, the captain doesn't know how they did it. They were literally carrying some of the guys who had passed out when they crossed. But the class finished the run in less than 30 minutes.

THE TAKE-AWAY

You want to be a senior vice president? You want to be a president? You want to be CEO? Know how to do it? Stand out as a team player. Do you think a solo star is what makes success? Wrong. And most of the time, companies recognize this.

There will always be the slimeball whom you'll watch in amazement as he or she continues to fail upward. Sorry—it happens. But other than in that unfortunate exception, the only position where only one person is important is called self-employment. Most companies—all quality organizations—recognize that everyone is dependent upon a team. The president, the CEO, the other senior executives, they're all supported closely by a team of people who help them make the right decisions every day. They are very aware of the value of team players. They are reminded every day that it's neither the cowboys nor the cogs, but the team players who drive success.

LESSON 8
YOU CAN'T FOOL PEOPLE
ABOUT BEING A TEAM PLAYER

THE MISSION

We were in a meeting in Latin America, listening to our commander introduce an ambitious, controversial plan for the region. The room was filled
with officers, chiefs, and leading petty officers. We all sat there silently.
The concept he envisioned had a big payoff, but it was loaded with some
pretty impressive obstacles. Everyone wanted to digest the scheme before
jumping on board. But after he finished, one of the officers piped up and
said, "Sound's great, sir."

The commander had an expression of slight puzzlement when he
looked at the enthusiastic young officer, and then he departed. As soon as
the door closed, the executive officer boomed, "Lieutenant so-and-so! Get
your nose out of the commander's rear!" I don't think anyone ever saw that
officer do that again.

THE TAKE-AWAY

Do you think people are stupid? Even 5-year-olds can spot the difference
between actors and real people. What makes you think that your boss,
who's been in the business for years, can't tell when you're just blowing
bubbles?

If you spend your time sucking up and playing at being a team member without doing the work, you'll waste a lot of time investing in a strategy that's eventually going to backfire on you.

Of course, this kind of nonsense goes on everywhere, from the SEALs
to corporate America. In Jon's pre-SEAL career, he was on a small team
that was perpetually swamped with work. In fact, every team in his division
was swamped with work. And to top it off, at that particular moment, they
were at the point in the month when each team had to pump out its peri-
odic productivity report.

It was a hellish scenario that we know is repeated everyday in some corner of the corporate world. Jon was furiously working on some reports that were due the following day, when he received an email message from a colleague that included something like the following:

> In the name of teamwork, could you please do the following pages of our report, which are normally done by so and so. So and so has an unusually large amount of work on his plate this week. Thanks.

It was impossible not to notice that copies of the message had been sent to Jon's boss, his colleague's boss, their boss, and all the other members of the team, presumably so that they would all know how much my colleague believed in the teamwork concept. Or maybe it was so that Jon would be aware that everyone's bosses and all the other team members were watching. He became depressed at the prospect of taking on even more of the load. But what could he do? It didn't matter that he was as swamped as everyone else. How could he refuse to do his work when the word teamwork had been invoked?

He talked to his boss, who now was also concerned about not appearing to be a team player, and who concluded the meeting by telling him to take on the extra pages.

In the end, Jon went to the guy who started this and told him that if he needed help in the future, to come in and ask him directly. *"Don't go to your boss and ask him to contact my boss when all you have to do is walk down the hall to my office."* Jon did the work—because he was told to. It was a clever way for the colleague to pass his load on to someone else while looking like a team player at the same time. But the next time he needed something, nobody stood up to give him a hand.

The take-away from this lesson is pretty simple: Don't play games in hopes of cutting corners, or currying favor with higher-ups, or maneuvering a situation to your advantage. These tactics may produce some short-term results, but while their benefits are fleeting, their fallout can be devastating. Other people know what you're up to, and they don't forget it, and someday they'll make you pay.

LESSON 9
THERE ARE PROBABLY GOOD REASONS WHY YOUR MARCHING ORDERS SEEM SCREWED UP

THE MISSION

During one training mission, we were trying to get out of bad-guy land quickly after picking up a downed aircrew on the run. A large number of opposing troops were following our trail. Our present course would soon bring us to a busy road, while to our left, a creek wound around in the same direction that we were traveling. I presumed that the troops behind us had radioed ahead that we were on the way. My best guess was that the road ahead would be a dangerous crossing. The opposing troops had vehicles and would be patrolling back and forth. Perhaps they already had an ambush ready.

On the other hand, the creek to our left was of unknown depth. Being caught in the middle of a river crossing would leave team members exposed and unprotected. And, of course, the act of crossing a river is simply far more difficult than that of crossing a road. The enemy knew this. Thus, they were probably assuming that we would head for the road.

We didn't have time to slow down. The enemy troops behind us were moving quickly, whereas we still had to move in a clandestine manner. I directed the point man down to the water, and the rest of the team followed. We set up a quick rear security group, and then the point man and his buddy stepped off the bank and into the current. Soon they were on the other side, and the next men went across with the pilots. None of us were comfortable about being spread out across the stream with the enemy so close. Right before the leading petty officer, a priceless wise guy, entered the water, he turned back to me, only half smiling, and said, "You know, a good platoon commander keeps his guys' feet dry."

He was half way across the water when an enemy soldier blundered into sight a hundred yards away and paused to rest. We all sank into the bushes. The leading petty officer froze in the middle of the stream. He was screwed. And the whole time he stayed there, he just stared at me, grinning. Even after the soldier moved on.

THE TAKE-AWAY

It was September back in the early 1990s, and Jeff was working on a $20 million piece of business for an agency. So when the agency's president told him to pull some of his people off the project to work on finding new business, he fought the decision. Why risk a good thing and start pulling back on our work? Why risk losing an existing client to start looking for new business? Sure, we all want growth. But what's the good of getting a new client just to lose the old one?

About a month later, he found out why. The regional client was in the process of being bought by a national company. It was great news for them, but bad news for Jeff's company. The president got the news over drinks with one of the client's executives. And although he couldn't talk about it, he knew what the writing on the wall was. By acting, he was a month ahead of the game, and the company was able to secure enough business to replace what was going to be lost.

Do you think you're right? Do you think you have the right answer? Have you ever thought that you don't know everything? If you're good, your answers are probably right. But half the time, you're probably making a decision in a partial vacuum. Have you ever thought that maybe you don't have all the information, and maybe, just maybe, your boss is making a decision because of info you don't have?

It's simple; the boss has the big picture. You don't. If you don't like the way he or she is leading, get out. If you don't like the project you're on, quit. But if you want to survive, you might just think of doing what the boss says.

LESSON 10
BUILD YOUR TEAM, BUILD YOUR RÉSUMÉ

THE MISSION

A fellow lieutenant's platoon was off Alaska, conducting a long-range transit in a small rubber boat in winter conditions. The icy waves were steep and high, causing the boats to jut up through the wintry swell and then crash back down. The outboard motors kept failing. Gas fumes hovered over the crews, making them ill as they held onto the lanyards to keep from being pitched over the side. Blasts of wind cut through their dry suits. It wasn't long before a torrent of hail and snow began, adding to the water that was already swamping their boats. And they were still hours and miles from their destination.

The radio bleeped from inside its layers and layers of waterproof plastic. The unit's headquarters wanted to know their status. Every hour that they fell behind increased their risk of not coming back at all. Fuel runs out fast. Disorientation and hypothermia can set in quickly. Helicopters can't always get to you. The fact that headquarters was contacting the platoon in the middle of a mission with such a basic question implied that it was concerned and was considering calling off the mission.

"We're good to go," one of the shivering SEALs boomed out. The lieutenant looked at the others as they volunteered equally cheery sentiments. "We're going to make this trip," the lieutenant said over the radio. End of story. Several SEAL demigods swayed back and forth at the other end of the radio, in a compartment of a larger ship that was itself rocking heavily in the seas. They controlled access to several megaprojects. They jotted down the names of the platoon members. They knew what kind of men were out there in the small boats, and they weren't going to forget who they were the next time an important mission came up.

THE TAKE-AWAY

How many of you have filled your résumé with things like "I did this," "I was responsible for sales of X," or "I produced these projects"? A lot of people do that. It shows how much they've accomplished individually. But it doesn't show what they've done as a team.

After looking at a lot of résumés and interviewing a lot of potential hires, you start to notice the difference. A résumé that talks about the person and not the team shows that the person views a job as just that, a job to be individually completed, not as a job to be completed as part of a team or a job to be completed in the service of a larger goal. And that is the perspective of someone who hasn't yet learned the importance of working within a team. That is the perspective of a person who is an employee and not a potential team leader.

How do successful leaders respond when someone congratulates them on a good job? They start talking about the great team they've got working for them. How this person or that person stepped up in the effort. Or how everyone really came together to pull through. Why? Because they know what it takes to succeed. It takes a team.

Nobody works in isolation. Your résumé is built on projects you've completed and successes you've been a part of. Any good manager knows that from experience. Don't downgrade your own contributions but rather than working solely to build a list of your own accomplishments, create a list of the larger accomplishments your efforts helped to build. Build the team you're on and you build your résumé.

LESSON 11
IT'S A SMALL WORLD,
AND IT'S GETTING SMALLER

THE MISSION

Word gets around in the SEAL teams. It's a small organization. Occasionally, there are applicants for the SEAL program who have strong political connections. The connections don't help an applicant get through the rigorous training program, but since there are limited opportunities to get in, the mere hint of a political connection invariably leads to the suspicion that strings have been pulled. And that's not a good thing to be associated with in a bust-your-gut meritocracy. Often, in fact, it's an unfair disadvantage.

Some time after I went through BUD/S, a candidate was coming into the program who made no secret of whom he knew. As we all knew, it's a tough program to get into. Lots of stellar athletes with top grades and high SEAL qualification scores get turned away. But he was quite open about his connections on his application. He had been a congressional aide. He had a letter of recommendation from a famous actor. A commander leading a discussion on the new candidates tried to counter the prejudices that were already crystallizing in our brains. "Guys, he's from such and such a university. A 4.0 grade point average. Captain of some team at the school. Extremely sharp. A real team player."

It didn't matter. "What's his name?" growled one of the BUD/S instructors, already planning the candidate's descent into hell.

On the darker side, I once worked on a team in which one of the SEALs became disenchanted with the standard SEAL workload necessary to keep the team moving. He worked in the dive locker, but he grew sloppy about inspecting diving rigs. He obviously stopped caring about gear maintenance, which translated into a lack of concern for his teammates. His leading petty officer tried to cover for him for a while, putting in extra work on his behalf. But the leading petty officer was never thanked, and the guy never made any attempt to refocus. The guy should have quit.

Years later, the leading petty officer had worked his way up and had gained an officer's commission. He ran the training cadre at one of the SEAL teams. One morning, one of his subordinates answered the phone in front of him, talked a little bit, and then turned toward the training officer. "It's petty officer so-and-so. He says he used to work for you back in the dive locker at another team. He wants to work here now."

"Tell him he is not welcome here," the training officer said simply.

THE TAKE-AWAY

Whom do you think you'll be working with in a few years? Do you think your peers will stay in the jobs they're currently in? Do you think you're going to be the only one advancing? If you do, think again.

Your team members are going to be with you for the rest of your life—in elevators or flight terminals, through email, and at cocktail parties, talking about you. Maybe some of them will drop out and do different things, but for the most part, the people you'll run into are the same people you started with, in one way or another. Think they'll have forgotten how you left the company with your project in tatters? Think again. Think local businesses will have forgotten how you stiffed them? No dice. There are so many good candidates out there. Often, one bad nudge is enough to place your résumé in the permanent round file. "No, don't worry. We're keeping it on file should everyone else on earth die."

On the other hand, when you work hard, do your job, and help others on your team, you'll make a lasting impression. People remember who was competent, who worked hard, who was fair, and who was their friend. People will remember when you came through.

Remember, often your future will irreparably be affected by a comment made far away, by someone you briefly knew a long time before. Make sure it's the right comment.

LESSON 12
THERE AREN'T MANY WAYS TO RADICALLY CHANGE A PROVEN SYSTEM

THE MISSION

SEALs in my platoons argued about whether they should put one shot into the head or two shots into the body. In the end, we all went for one head shot, followed by the body shots. In terms of modifying techniques or equipment, that was about as deep as it went. We customized a few systems in order to align them more closely with the way we did business, but that was it—they weren't big changes. Most of the SEAL procedures we used had been developed and proven under fire long before we arrived on the scene. For the SEALs, these are the equivalent of the Ten Commandments. They're called Standard Operating Procedures (SOPs).

That's not to say that the SEAL organization rests on its procedural laurels. Other systems are always being explored and developed by training cells within the teams. Better systems are still out there, waiting to be discovered, tested, and designated as new SOPs. But they have to be demonstrably superior in order to replace the existing procedures.

For example, the techniques for assaulting a building have been in place for years. SEAL platoons that train in this capability spend months getting it down right, and with good reason. An assault is an opportunity to capture something important or kill someone at relatively close range. That means whoever you're assaulting can shoot back. If something small goes the other way, the momentum of the assault can be irretrievably turned against you. I'll say it again: The bad guys can shoot back. They can run out the back and run around and attack you from the rear. They can lock and booby-trap doors and toilets and refrigerator doors. And then your team will start taking hits. For these reasons, SEAL instructors have no tolerance for divergence from SOPs.

When my platoon trained for an assault, we did so with all of the successful and flawed assaults of the past in mind. The time a platoon didn't clear the entire room but left a bad guy in the corner. The time guys stayed too close to the walls. The time a guy went into the next room too fast without someone behind him. There are proven reasons why commandos enter and move through a building in a certain way. The gang that decides to bypass the current system, that simply sticks guns in the door and begins firing, does so only after ignoring the generations of experience that preceded it. And once you've disregarded those generations of experience and made a mess of things, it will be only a matter of time before there's one more lesson that's passed down to future generations—the lesson about how not to do whatever it is you've just done.

THE TAKE-AWAY

So much emphasis has been placed on entrepreneurship, "thinking outside the box," and "the New Economy" that the importance of adhering to an accepted system has often been glossed over. There's a great line from the movie *Swimming with Sharks*. It goes something like this: "If you don't rebel against the system when you're 24, you'll never amount to anything, and if you're not a part of it by the time you're 30, you'll never do anything."

"The system" is a dreaded term that a large part of the workforce apparently hates, fears, and loathes. It's the stuff of books, movies, and canned campus demonstrations. *Fight against the system, you rebel, you!* Yet, for better or worse, every organization has one. Some are good. Some are mired in bureaucracy. And some are barely noticed. But whichever kind you end up with, you're not going to get away from it. It's that simple.

If you think you can just walk in and ignore or change the system, think again, even if your last name is on the side of the building. Right now, the Ford Motor Company has a pretty established way to produce automobiles. The problem is that while that system used to be extremely profitable, it's probably not producing the bucks the way it used to. Something has to change. So, recently, a young member of the Ford family took the helm of the Ford Motor Company. He has the name. He has the backing of the board. He has a plan to bring the company around. Do you think he's going to simply throw a switch and overturn everything the company built and disrupt how things have been done by thousands of people over the course of several years? That would cause more harm than good. He's already making changes. But they're most likely changes that fit into the existing system, augmenting it, improving it, building for a longer-term solution.

We know that we're probably not telling you what you'd like to hear. We know you'd rather we told you that part of project leadership is being a maverick, that being a leader means bravely bucking the system. Champions of change for change's sake. There are times when a company must be painfully wrenched out of the past and set on a new course. It's often a jolting, searing experience full of risk and uncertainty with which expressions like "dissatisfaction" and "layoffs" and "pay cuts" are associated. If it's done just so you can wear the big hat and bandana, that's not leadership. That's being a cowboy.

Often, doing what's right means taking the less dramatic road of supporting the company's long-term goals, and then doing your part to bring the efforts of the people under you into harmony with those goals. Sometimes the system itself gets in the way of those goals. But unless you're the top dog and have a real chance of changing the system, and the costs of changing the system are worth the benefits, your job is to continue to work within its current framework toward those long-term goals. As time goes by, the more credibility you gain, the better your chances of effecting meaningful change. But no matter what you do, or what your level is, it's not going to happen overnight. So if you can't stand the system you're in, you're better off hunting for a new one than frustrating yourself, your team, and your boss by trying to lead a revolution. Hey, Ché Guevera caps are sexy, but sometimes revolutions are only good in songs. Know the difference.

LESSON 13
OWN EVERYTHING YOU DO

THE MISSION

There was a SEAL candidate at BUD/S who just didn't seem to give a damn. It showed up in all sorts of ways. Once, during a dive, he was too tired to confirm the bearing of our dive headings. We hit the shallow water before we finally recognized what had happened, reversed course, and somehow found our way to the target. During land navigation, he didn't take the time to include magnetic declination when he plotted his land navigation course. The courses were miles long and took hours and sometimes days to complete. We climbed an additional peak because of his inattention, reached base camp during late morning instead of early morning, and missed our opportunity to sleep before our next assignment.

But it could have been worse. Instead of heading toward shore, the wrong dive bearing could have put the squad under the wrong ship. Perhaps it would have put us under a ship that was too large to swim out from under with all of our equipment. Perhaps one of us would have become trapped in one of the suction vents that pull in seawater to cool the engines. Perhaps our air would have run out before we realized we were off course. All of these were possible outcomes of his negligence—it's just dumb luck that none of them actually happened.

The thing is, it would have taken him only a few minutes to check his numbers and prevent a potential casualty. By not taking those few additional minutes, he had decided that our lives were not of sufficient importance for him to bother checking for mistakes. That chance to eliminate unnecessary risk from a potentially hazardous dive didn't warrant a few additional minutes of his time. This guy didn't go on to become a SEAL.

THE TAKE-AWAY

You've got a job. By being there, you've accepted that job. You have specific things to do. And if you fail at those things, a lot of other people are going to have to pay the price. Yeah, we know. You're better than that glamour kid next to you. Yeah, we know. You have so much more to offer. Yeah, we know, we're lucky to have a genius like you working for us. We're all surprised you haven't taken one of those many offers that are probably on your desk right now.

Well, guess what. You may be smart, but if you don't take ownership of the work at hand, everyone else is going to have to pay for what you didn't do. Then, everyone is going to blame you, no matter how many facts, figures, and points of interest you can remember at one time. No matter what your aunt's maiden name was. No matter how much you know about the French impressionists.

All your talent and smarts will pay off in time. But if you've got a job, pay attention to what you're doing now or go somewhere else to work. Anyone can find someone to daydream and dawdle for free.

LESSON 14
SWEAT THE SMALL RITUALS

THE MISSION

SEAL teams conduct uniform inspections. There is no direct correlation between the amount of starch in summer whites and the ability to shoot a moving target at a thousand yards. However, the care given to a uniform and the crispness with which a salute is rendered are direct indicators of professionalism, attention to detail, and adherence to a warfare culture. And there is a direct correlation between *these* and the ability to shoot well.

One of my missions was to assess the ability of foreign militaries to conduct operations with U.S. commandos. In many countries, esprit de corps and professionalism was alive and well, even despite small budgets and low standards of living. On the other hand, in several countries where I worked, it was evident that the local soldiers didn't have the discipline to stand in ranks or the means or willingness to maintain their uniforms, or even to shave. It's significant that even I noticed this, since commandos are notorious for their nonregulation haircuts, and couldn't stand in a proper formation if their lives depended on it. In these countries, however, the extent of neglect, the disparities between uniforms, and the lack of simple formalities in front of their leaders implied that this was not simply a casual day at headquarters. This was the accepted standard.

Understandably, this caused the members of my team some concern. Would the same standard that allowed for their lax appearance and disposition also carry over to more important things—their weapons, for example? Invariably, if I picked up one of their rifles and slid a cotton swab around its gun chamber, it would come out greasy and black. In one country, no one showed up on time for a morning meeting. Later, a soldier began firing his machine gun at a target, oblivious or unconcerned that his teammates were still wandering across the range. Would their lackadaisical attitude continue on the battlefield? Would their indifference to what their leaders said while in ranks translate into a lack of respect for their experienced chiefs and petty officers in the field? Was there any kind of dependable organizational structure that would make a difference in a firefight?

We returned from many of these countries with the recommendation that joint training between our two organizations not be conducted. Simple things like poorly maintained uniforms had led to the discovery of more serious conditions. And remember, this is coming from a guy who has spent most of his professional life wearing a swimsuit to work.

THE TAKE-AWAY

This lesson is about how the little things that seem pretty frivolous and unimportant can actually hurt you in profound and unexpected ways. It doesn't just apply to keeping your weapon clean—corporate America has its own version of this lesson. For example, a company Jeff worked for had just won a new assignment, so he trucked out to the client's headquarters to meet with the people there and get to work. During this meeting, the client's people mentioned the proposals. And one of the things that really stood out for them was the fact that pictures of the team had been included with the proposals. To them, this small thing was indicative of a company that thought of itself as a family and held those implied values in high regard. It was the kind of people that the client wanted to work with.

Do you think this doesn't make sense? Okay, suppose you're in an investment firm. People pay you a lot of money to make sure their money is being handled with the greatest care. Many of them don't want a lot of high-flying talk of imaginative accounting and complicated financial maneuvering. They want to make sure that at the end of the day, they're going to have more money than they started with. They want to see a conservative person in a suit and tie who watches every penny they've saved for their children's education.

Or maybe you're in a design shop and the last thing anyone wants to see is a conservative suit; instead they want to see a person whose unique or creative style of dress practically screams ideas, ideas, ideas. It may seem like nonsense, but who's to say that dressing that way doesn't actually help the company be more creative. People want the real thing and they have a certain preconceived notion of what the real thing is. And dressing down at a design shop might reinforce that notion.

So get with the program. Organizations have rituals because those rituals are part of how the organization does business. Wearing a tie may represent profitability and reliability, which is important when dealing with certain customers. A regulation haircut may signify adherence to a professional culture. Using an accepted memo format may signify familiarity with accepted regulations. Repeating a simple phrase may strengthen feelings of membership.

By maintaining its rituals, an organization is communicating the idea that a system or culture is in place. By adhering to its rituals, you are confirming that you belong to the organization. If you buck the system, you are not simply rebelling against formal suits and orthodox memos; you are questioning the organization, strategies, and processes they represent. You are questioning the company you work for.

So get over it. It's not just about you. A client that has hired the company you work for isn't just hiring you. It's hiring everything that your company represents. And if you don't believe in what your company represents, then why are you there? When it comes time to promote someone, whom do you think the company is going to want as a leader? Someone who believes in what the company's about, or someone who's just along for the ride?

This isn't about being a suck-up and doing what someone else wants. It's about working for a company that you believe in—through and through.

LESSON 15
BRING ME THE PROBLEM
ALONG WITH A SOLUTION

THE MISSION

I was in the Middle East with a platoon when the platoon commander came into my tent with some bad news. "We don't have all of the ammunition we're supposed to have," he told me. "Some of it that was supposed to come in on the flight this morning never arrived." I was concerned, but he interrupted me.

"I've already called the unit that was supposed to send it," he continued. "I have two of my guys going to the airstrip in case it was accidentally sent there. In the meantime, the Special Forces company in town can lend us what we need. In either case, we should know where our ammo is, shortly. And we'll still have what we need in case we get tasked with a mission."

There it was. There was no complaining. No simply dumping of a problem. What my platoon commander was really doing was informing me that he was taking care of a problem. And there's no better indicator of leadership than someone who is willing to solve a problem.

THE TAKE-AWAY

You want respect? Then make sure you give that same respect to your boss. Don't waste your boss's time by presenting a problem and then dumping it in his or her lap.

If there's a problem, make sure you've thought about it enough to come up with a solution. Is something broken? Tell us how you're going to fix it. Is a client angry? Tell us how you want to make nice. If you don't work through it on your own, what makes you think someone's going to give you the responsibility for it in the future?

If you want to grow, you need to prove you can handle your current job. And that means having a solution for the problems you're encountering. If you don't have a solution ready, or if you feel you're unable to generate a solution, or if you aren't able to communicate the problem to your people so that you can tap their expertise, then maybe you're not someone who can handle the job. And that's not a good thing as far as moving up is concerned.

Oh, and if you're bringing up a problem as a way of complaining, that just wastes everyone's time. So go kick your dog instead.

CHAPTER 5

BUILDING A
THUNDERING HERD

THE WAY IT IS

How often have you heard something like the following?

- "Does accounting even know what business we're in? Do they realize that they're the support group for us, not the other way around?"

- "It's only six o'clock, and it's already a ghost town on the fifth floor. I thought they were going to stay to help us on this."

- "We ought to make this company like the Marine Corps. At least they know which side to shoot at."

- "Who was the idiot that hired that one, and why is he still here?"

Unless the people who make these comments are actively pursuing changes in their companies, they are woefully nearsighted. A good work ethic doesn't come into being with a morning cup of coffee. Strong professional bonds aren't suddenly created during a 2-day team-building session in the woods. A culture that promotes stringent quality controls isn't produced just because the boss started screaming after a product recall.

If you haven't guessed by now, organizations don't suddenly become great because all at once someone decides to require excellence. Organizations become great because they foster excellence over time. It's the same with the teams within these organizations. It takes time to build good ones.

Nonetheless, many managers are frustrated by what they see as a corporate failure to provide them with the highly skilled workers and sharp, energetic executives that they believe they deserve. It's an easy out to say, "We don't have the right people." It's a lot tougher to look at the team today and decide how to build a stronger team for tomorrow.

Strong organizations are built or revised from the ground up, and then continually strengthened over time. If you want something strong in the future, start now. By the time you're finished, you may look around and realize that the great company you used to fantasize about working for is a reality.

LESSON 1
DO YOU REALLY WANT TO BUILD A QUALITY TEAM?

THE MISSION

We were in the Southern Hemisphere, working on an operation with the local commandos. Our counterparts stared at the 80-pound packs we carried. "We don't need that stuff," one of them suddenly threw out. "We know how to survive on the local environment." He nodded toward a village that we were passing—his idea of the local environment.

As we worked with this group and others like it, we noticed that they really weren't into the hardships that come with being a commando. For many of them, physical fitness was a totally abstract concept. You'd be hard-pressed to get them to hike a few miles. Their stomachs hung out over their belts. Forget about their being able to do a few chin-ups, let alone enough to get up the side of a tall ship.

Others had very little discipline. We could drive right through the gates of their main bases, and if we'd had a bomb, we could easily have taken out many of their senior officers or aircraft. No one asked us for identification. Sometimes the guard would poke his head up over the windowsill to see who was driving by. Other times he remained out of sight.

One of the senior officers in one of these troubled organizations complained to me, "I tell my men that they must stop you and ask you for your identification. And they tell me yes. And then I see you drive right past them and they do nothing. And I tell them again that they have to stop you. And they say yes again. But I know they will not stop you. They think you are fine because you are American. They don't understand that that's not the point."

He would have been more accurate if he had simply said, "My guys ignore me because they know they can, and that's not going to change."

But I suspect that the casual tempo of his organization better suited his countrymen. The alternative would have meant sweating and being in the field and getting wet and cold. Why should they do things like that, which are unpopular with their troops, when they could get U.S. commandos to do those things for them?

Military organizations in many countries aren't interested in building high-quality teams. They want well-equipped ones. They like the idea of having fighter planes, and missiles, and soldiers who march well in great uniforms. But maintenance, and hard work? That's something else. I once worked in a country with a huge fleet of transport vehicles. During one exercise to test their response capabilities, a third of their vehicles never left the parking lot. Why? Simple things like fan belts being worn out, tires being flat, and motors having no oil. Months, maybe years, had gone by since the vehicles had been last serviced. Today, many governments continue to purchase top-of the-line equipment, weapons, and communications gear. They see movies and read books about what we have done and continue to do, and they like what they see. They want to socialize with us. Many of them have modern headquarters, usually with leather furniture, models of ships and airplanes, and walls covered with plaques from foreign military units and dignitaries. And every one of their senior officers wants to send several of their troops to a commando school in the United States.

But what good will that do them if the organization at home is perfectly content with mediocrity?

THE TAKE-AWAY

Being good is tough. It means performing at a higher level than your competitors. It means constantly being on guard. And, of course, there is no free lunch. If you want a good team and a good organization, start providing heavily in terms of training, morale building, bonding, and discipline.

To meet your toughest requirements, throwing money at your team will not be enough. Several countries with lousy commando teams have per capita incomes that are comparable to that of the United States. Meanwhile, commandos in Latvia, Chile, Colombia, Romania, Poland, Peru and many other developing economies are professional, organized, disciplined, fit, and ready to do business.

Your greatest problem will be raising the standards from what you have now. Enforcing a higher work ethic. Increasing morale through increased hardships. That means being the bad guy at first. That means getting rid of the people who don't fit in. That means demanding more than people are used to giving. And if you're doing this because you're looking for a group of lifelong friends, think again. That's a nice perk, not the objective. Are you sure you're up for the job? Or do you just enjoy talking about what should be done at your company while you hang out with your subordinates at the water cooler?

LESSON 2
CONTINUALLY SET HIGH STANDARDS

THE MISSION

SEALs must first graduate from BUD/S. There is no other way to become a naval commando. And in order to graduate, they must be able to run far and fast through drifting sand, swim for miles in the frigid ocean, master an assortment of equipment and weapons, dive in arduous conditions, and conduct intense team-based operations. They also have to prove that they'll never, never, never quit. No matter what.

Before being placed on a SEAL team, a BUD/S graduate must graduate from parachute jump school and advanced SEAL training. While they are on a team, SEALs must routinely pass physical conditioning tests. Before a platoon can be deployed, it must pass a series of arduous training courses and qualification tests, culminating in an extended, realistic, full-profile contingency simulation.

All these are requirements. They are not negotiable. A commander of an operation in a future war will never direct a platoon that has not met these standards. He will never have under his command individual SEALs who have not passed their individual requirements.

THE TAKE-AWAY

If you want a team that works, you need to do a lot more than just hire competent folks and then sit back while they automatically excel. You need to continuously work with your team to determine what they're capable of accomplishing. This entails finding their weak spots and fixing them until their goals are met, and then raising the bar to a new level. Then making that new bar the standard.

Setting a high standard is not about accomplishing a superior objective and then backing off. A large number of workers can occasionally produce fantastic results, with large dry spells in between. A large portion of the population can walk the distance of a marathon, and then not walk again for a long time. A lot of sailors and soldiers can occasionally hit a bull's eye, firing lots of stray bullets in between. When your team occasionally does produce a fantastic result, congratulations! It has done something extraordinary. The team members have done something that they couldn't do every day. The down side, of course, is that they perceive it as an unusual achievement, one that cannot be accomplished every day. You reinforce that perception every time you thank them for doing something exceptional. *"Thanks for getting the project in on time, guys. That was really unusual."*

Setting a high standard means that your team will shine day after day, because it won't see it as shining. Team members will see it as what's expected of them. Every week, when SEALs go for a routine sand run or ocean swim, they don't finish up and think, "Wow! I just did what few Americans do!" Instead, they look around at how they did compared to their teammates. Simply running and swimming was the bare minimum.

When your team accepts what used to be superior as a routine standard, then you're on your way. Although your team members will regard their standards as ordinary, they'll know that they are far above the accepted standards of other teams. One SEAL captain used to call this the "golden key." "Deep down inside, I know that I am able to continuously perform far beyond what I ever thought I could."

LESSON 3

RETAIN YOUR BEST PEOPLE OR YOU'LL PAY THROUGH THE NOSE

THE MISSION

One day, after a 10-year career, a friend of mine who ran SEAL operations in Europe quit. In doing so, he cost the American taxpayer over a million dollars. Within a year of his resignation, more than 50 other SEAL officers resigned, enough officers to lead every SEAL platoon currently deployed on operations. That's tens of millions of lost dollars. And then there were the hundreds of enlisted SEAL operators who left as well.

Today, the United States is dangerously short of commandos. This is because of the bleeding away that's been going on over the last decade combined with the enormous demand for them today. The bleeding was noticeable when I was stationed overseas for 5 years, in Latin America and in Europe. During that time, I worked with small groups of SEALs who were forward deployed as regional experts for the SEAL organization.

That these SEALs had an unusually high rate of separation from the Navy was surprising at first, given our circumstances. After all, we were living overseas, something most Americans can only dream about, and most SEAL overseas destinations are either exotic locations or sophisticated capitals and cultural centers. We were the closest SEALs in the organization to any war, conflict, or contingency that arose, which was a big plus. And my peers were fellow veterans in the commando community. They were tight, experienced groups of professionals who had spent many years as operators before taking on this role. It was a great working environment. So what went wrong?

Well, despite these attractions, there were several dark issues hovering beneath the surface. First, SEALs stationed overseas began to perceive that in terms of career advancement, they were losing out to their peers who had stayed stateside. We assumed that while we shuttled from country to country, our peers back home were sidling up to the admiral and getting the plum future jobs.

Also, SEALs working overseas were more likely to feel profound political or bureaucratic frustration. Operations overseas frequently involved coordination with staffs from the State Department, NATO, or large U.S. military commands, and in such discussions we were likely to be the most junior person in the room. Meanwhile, the discrepancy between political promises and actual results on the ground was apparent to anyone who traveled in and out of conflict areas, and that led to a loss of faith and even depression. Everyone overseas knew what was actually happening in Bosnia, regardless of what the press reported.

Finally, forward-deployed SEALs were older and more experienced than the rest, and thus were more likely to be married and have families. Isolated tropical locales rapidly lose their luster when kids get sick, electricity and telephones are shut off without warning, no work or support system is available for spouses, schools aren't up to par, and the natives turn unfriendly.

The result was a rash of resignations. Worse still, those who resigned were experienced midlevel SEALs with years of corporate knowledge and combat experience under their belts.

The cost of retaining these SEALs would have been relatively small. Some issues, such as national politics, couldn't have been helped. But better overseas medical facilities and living conditions would have had a big impact. Job and language assistance for spouses would have helped. Keeping my buddy in the organization would have cost the U.S. taxpayer, at most, a couple of thousand dollars more.

On the other hand, losing him meant spending hundreds of thousands of dollars in salary over 10 years, hundreds of thousands of dollars in training, and hundreds of thousands of dollars in equipment and travel costs in order to develop another officer. And it would be years before this process was completed and that replacement officer could fulfill all the responsibilities that my friend gave up when he walked out the door.

In addition, this was a guy who had been around the world and was deeply respected. He was a leader. His resignation was a signal to the rest of the organization that something was wrong. Other SEALs were shocked when they heard about it. His departure planted the seeds for other resignations and removed many other promising senior officers from the SEAL organization.

THE TAKE-AWAY

Hiring good people is a 2-month process at best and is often costly no matter what the organization does. You need to put ads in the various media. You need to interview. You need to check credentials. And the people you hire need several weeks to let their current employers know they're leaving. If you're using a headhunter to speed up the process, you're going to have to pay for it. And if you're not, then you'll need to spend even more time searching for good people. In the end, the final choice you make is always a bit of a crapshoot. Worse still, the person you're bringing in needs to learn the ropes and tricks of your organization. And that takes time.

On the other hand, growing your existing employees costs relatively little when compared to going outside. By keeping those you have, you'll continue to know whom you're dealing with, and whom your clients are dealing with. Moreover, by investing in your people, you'll reinforce their loyalty.

There are many valid reasons for bringing in outside people: Your current workers are not sufficiently competent. You need more of them. Or you need a breath of fresh air. Rarely can you deliver a solution to these problems by going in-house. But there is an enormous cost to going outside. If you have an opportunity to keep the woman who excels at her job, don't ignore the conditions that might make her jump ship.

The take-away here is that if you have good people, then you need to train them, improve them, and grow them. You need to listen to what they want and need and then deliver it. And if you can't deliver it, you need to explain why, and let them know what both of you need to do to work toward that goal. That's part of the deal. That's your responsibility. If you're not doing it, then you need to reconsider how badly you want your team to succeed. And if you decide you don't want the team members to succeed badly enough, then don't expect them to stay. In retention, you're either with them or you're against them. If you're not actively trying to keep and grow your people, then you're pushing them away. And that is a waste of your most valuable resource.

LESSON 4
IF YOU'RE HIRING, MAKE THEM COME TO YOU

THE MISSION

This is an account of a real SEAL mission:

> Here was a real nice insertion we did: We jumped into the Pacific right at sunset. The edge of the sea bisected the setting red sun when the ramp doors opened. We were flying so low—low enough to stay below the horizon—that you could see the veins of bright white surf fragmenting the dark blue water below us. It was beautiful. In the half-second after splashing down, when we

looked back up toward the surface through the rushing bubbles and swirling canopy squares, the water was sweet and clear. Then everyone was out of his harness and swimming to the rubber boats, which had been parachuted down as well. And then everyone was on board the boats, shaking dry, just as the edge of the sea swallowed up the sun completely.

To our west, a speck of island rose out of the enormous blue ocean. Dark volcanic cliffs jutted up directly from the water. The only break in the cliffs, according to the map, was a small natural inlet that led into a small lagoon. A small path wound up the side of the cliff from the lagoon. Anyone waiting would know that this was the single route to the top of the cliffs. But taking the surprise route—climbing the cliffs directly from the sea—wouldn't leave us enough time to travel far enough inland before light. Nor could we infiltrate in on the opposite side of the island, which didn't have cliffs, because that's where all the towns and resorts lay, along with their thousands of inquisitive eyes. By dropping at sunset, we had almost 9 nighttime hours to transit to the inlet and get far enough inland to hide out before sunlight, so that we could reach our target by the following night.

LT XXXXX
SEAL platoon commander
199X

As countless SEALs have joked during long ocean swims, tall ice climbs in Norway, or treks through the upper Amazon, "Some people have to pay to do this."

If you want to do these things for a living, you know where to go. Why? Because the SEAL organization, through its operations, has firmly established the word *SEAL* as meaning something powerful. It conjures up images of adventure and excitement. It's what some people know they need, deep down inside.

Ask guys why they're trying to get into the program. They'll tell you that being a SEAL means fighting for one's country, being part of an extremely close-knit team, traveling around the world, receiving the best training in the world, handling boatloads of responsibility, and achieving truly amazing goals that most people can only dream of.

That is an accurate perception.

Ask them why they want to become SEALs when they could have a higher-paying job with less work somewhere else. They'll repeat themselves. Fighting for one's country, being part of an extremely close-knit team, traveling around the world, receiving the best training in the world, handling boatloads of responsibility, and achieving truly amazing goals that most people can only dream of.

Where else are they going to go?

THE TAKE-AWAY

What organization do you want to work for? Microsoft? Procter & Gamble? Joe Roth's Revolution Studios? Amazon.com? Why? Chances are, even before you started doing your research, you perceived them as embodying something you wanted to be part of.

How much do you really know about any organization before you actually start working there? Probably not much, and what you do know is probably based more on what you've heard than on the facts. It's no different for anyone else. Everyone wants to work for the exciting company that's in the news. Nobody wants to work for a company whose stock is tanking, except for a turn-around artist.

If you want to hire the best people, attract them before you start interviewing. Public relations isn't just about adding value to the stock price. It's about promoting your organization to potential employees. Push the benefits of your company with the press. Let people know how great you are before you even consider placing a want ad. If you do your PR correctly, you'll never have to place that ad. You'll simply have to go through the stacks of résumés you've been collecting, or open the door to the line of applicants outside.

LESSON 5
YOUR OWN PEOPLE ARE
YOUR BEST RECRUITERS

THE MISSION

On my last deployment, we carried a box of generic information about the SEAL organization. The SEAL organization is always looking for potential SEALs because there's a lot of work to go around. One of the best places to find them is in the rest of the Navy. Young sailors already have security clearances and technical skills. They're patriotic and in good physical shape, and they understand chains of command, teamwork, and personal deference to the larger mission. They're more likely to be informed about the SEAL mission and job description than their civilian counterparts.

Because many people are already attracted to the idea of being a SEAL, we don't have to spend much time trying to sell the program. Instead, our primary recruiting goal is to determine who the best candidates are, educate them on how they can enter the SEAL program, and motivate them to actually do so.

Using the guys in the platoon to do this is one of the most effective methods. They can instantly pick up on the difference between the liars and those who are truly sincere in their desire to join. Platoon members can talk from experience about how the SEALs operate and can minutely describe day-to-day scenarios. They aren't official recruiters, so what they say is taken at face value. Some of them have served on ships themselves and can relate directly to their audience of crew members.

We often ran operations from destroyers and cruisers, where it would soon become apparent to the crews that SEALs were on board. They would see us planning ship attacks or climbing over the gunwale. Mature, squared-away, fit guys with cool weapons and equipment. Curious gunner's mates, cooks, hull technicians, and ensigns began to cautiously come forward. The platoon guys fielded their questions in corridors, described missions over games of checkers in the mess hall, and showed them their equipment before storing it away below decks. Some of the crews were given rides on the fast boats we operated. They also gave us their names and identification numbers for us to pass on.

Do the SEALs recruit? 24/7.

THE TAKE-AWAY

Go to a college or MBA recruiting event and watch whom the companies that recruit most successfully bring along. They bring their recent college or MBA graduates, probably from the college or MBA program that they're visiting. These graduates may not know everything about the company they work for yet, but they can relate to and communicate with prospective hires better than anyone else at the company.

Who are your best recruiters? Your own people, the ones who really believe in what they are doing and who see the opportunities. These are the people you want up front and personal. Not just at campus recruitment events, but in the classrooms, giving seminars, hosting events, and talking to interns.

If your company is looking for new people, send someone who best reflects your organization to a networking event or chamber of commerce meeting. Let others see and talk with that person. Get the word out about what kind of company you are, at the grassroots level.

If you depend on sexy presentations, fine dinners, and shiny gifts to compete against a bunch of other recruiters for possible hires, you've given up a huge advantage. The recruits you want are smart enough to know what a free dinner represents in the recruiting process. They want to know what kind of company you have. Give them the dinner, but also let them see and talk with people like them who are already working for you.

LESSON 6
GIVE REAL REWARDS FOR REAL ACHIEVEMENTS

THE MISSION

The only person who knows what a medal is worth is the person receiving it. Staffers in the U.S. embassy in Jerusalem got Bronze Stars during the Gulf War. Commandos who swam over and sank 1000-pound mines before they hit their ship received a slap on the back. Which was worth more? Only the guy getting it pinned on has the real story.

During the later phases of BUD/S, my class screwed up an evolution and the instructors asked me for the names of those whom I considered responsible. We were in the diving portion of training at the time. We prepared for our dives in the morning, working in a wide-open section of the compound that was filled with equipment racks and rows of oxygen bottles. I didn't give them anything. Instead, I said I was responsible, and I was told to go get in the dip tank. I'm sure they knew I was lying.

The dip tank, a large steel tub used for washing salt and sediment off of dive gear, was filled with icewater at the time. The sun had just come up, and the air was still cold. Some of our T-shirts were still wet from the previous night's dive. I sat down in the tub quickly and sucked in my stomach. The rest of the class was brought around and put in the push-up position around the tank.

The instructors pointed at me and barked at them to look at what was happening to me because I wouldn't give up anyone else. *Get it? Everyone recognize what he's doing for you.* That made my day.

I had a junior officer on my staff during part of my last deployment. Like the rest of us, he was a vampire, pulling night shifts every time a mission was going down. But he also worked all day. He ran half a dozen platoons and detachments on land while I was out on the ship. He sheltered us from the base commander and ran interference with the locals. As a result, I called our bosses, swore that this guy was the Second Coming, and begged them to extend him to me. The medal write-up was incidental.

The real reward I gave him was when I told all the other commandos that he was in charge.

THE TAKE-AWAY

Do your rewards only involve pay, stock options, or a corner office? They shouldn't, because that's not what people want on a day-to-day basis. What they want is honest, straightforward feedback. When they've done something well, they want to be recognized for it. They want loyalty from those above them. They want a leader who will stick up for them and take the same abuse and punishment that they get.

A friend was recently transferred to a different division in his company. A few weeks after he left, we talked. He seemed unhappy. Why? He admitted that he had wanted his former boss to throw a small send-off for him. Nothing big. Maybe just a few sodas and they would stand around talking. He was embarrassed about wanting something so petty. His company should be the one embarrassed. It would have cost them almost nothing.

LESSON 7
IDENTIFY YOUR LEAD DOGS, FEED THEM WELL, AND BUILD A PACK AROUND THEM

THE MISSION

Find yourself a good chief. Building a platoon is a competitive business, and you need someone with a big paddle in the water. Why? Because while you're up there in the clouds, strategizing about how to get your platoon employed, you need someone back on earth actually holding the fort. In a short amount of time, you will have to gather 15 wild dogs and make them into the most harmonious unit in the universe. That means mixing and matching different personalities, different specialties, different experiences, and different physiologies. And at the same time, you'll be competing against other platoons for missions. To be successful, you need a guy who can put a firm hand on one of the kids' shoulders while you're out talking with the skipper.

When I was first told that I would be commanding a platoon, I went hunting for the best chief I could find. Of those that were available, there was one in particular that all the future platoon commanders were trying to recruit. I went directly to the team's executive officer, who handles organization and personnel issues, and pleaded my case. "Sir, most of my guys are brand spanking new and just out of BUD/S. I need somebody strong who can corral the thundering herd." Another platoon commander, who was also looking for a chief, heard what I was saying and jumped into the room. But it was too late. The executive officer gave me the chief I wanted. After we walked out of the executive officer's office, the other platoon commander asked me whom I had snagged, and I told him. "Damn," he said and hurled the book he was reading to the ground.

I also struck gold with my leading petty officer, or LPO, the next in line after the chief. Here's what happens when you have a good LPO: The platoon commander makes the plan. The chief makes it a workable plan. And then the LPO charges forward and actually gets his peers to carry out the plan. The guy I got was brilliant, and an animal. If you told him you needed a forklift at a port in Japan while you were standing on the quay, he'd suddenly appear with one. No questions asked.

Filling the rest of the platoon required some math. Because of other deployments and operations at the time, there were only a few SEALs available who had prior deployments under their belts. But there were lots of guys right out of BUD/S. I had only two deployments and one war under my belt myself at the time, so no matter how I cut it, we'd have a lot of new guys on the platoon.

No matter. I modeled my strategy after the official SEAL plan. My chief and my LPO were to be the core of my platoon, with one of them in each squad. I kept them in the intelligence loop. Every order went through them. I backed up their decisions. I let the rest of the platoon know that these two spoke on my behalf.

After we'd been together for a short time, my guys proved to be gods who could perform marvels. Another platoon was stuffed with experienced veterans but had a lousy chief and a troublemaker of an LPO. They self-destructed at meetings, bickered in the field, and sat in their rooms stewing. Their deployment was very long and very painful.

THE TAKE-AWAY

We've seen the same approach work in corporate America. When you first come in, there's an existing group of people on the team. Some of them have been around for a while; some are new and eager. And it's rarely those with the titles that really lead the teams.

Once, when being brought in to lead a group, the person that everyone came to for direction had the lowest title. After watching this, it seemed a promotion and a raise were in order to officially give her all the responsibilities that everyone was already heaping on her. Another time, someone had to be fired. The individual had a great title but was the monkeywrench in the works and would continue to be so.

Do either of these actions sound easy? They weren't easy at all. They meant fighting with a lot of people to convince them that the true leaders weren't the ones in the key positions. Did these actions create the teams needed? It was a start. By putting the best people in the key positions, it made everyone respect what we were doing. It made other employees want to join us because they sensed that things were changing in our group. It also gave everyone the feeling that leadership opportunities would be based on skill and talent, rather than on relationships. That goes a long, long way toward establishing a quality team.

LESSON 8
FIND OUT WHAT MAKES THEM TICK

THE MISSION

During the waning days of Pol Pot, my platoon was on call to rescue any idiot tourists who happened to be in Cambodia. We were given our warning order, which outlines what we should prepare for. A warning order basically states that a serious situation is at hand, that your team is being considered as an option should the United States decide to respond to this emergency, and that you should ensure that your team is ready to operate. Then we had an in-depth intelligence briefing.

The briefer was going over probable courses of action by the Khmer Rouge when I heard a loud nasal exhalation to my right. I looked over. One of my 50-caliber machine gunners, a mountain of a man from North Carolina, spit out a sunflower seed and nodded. The briefer began going into detail about the rules of engagement that we could use while taking out bands of kidnappers and terrorists. "Yeah, baby," the mountain said. The briefer went into the other organizations and support elements that would be put into play to support our mission. This was it. The possibility of an actual mission. The rest of the platoon was getting caught up in it as well. This is what they came here for—to kick down doors, shoot bad people, and rescue Americans in trouble.

A platoon needs continuous reminders that it is doing something important, commandolike, and real. The SEAL organization's job is to get it what it needs. I spent my time hunting for missions. I beseeched my boss to find us a mission. Have to feed the dogs! Have to feed the dogs! It's a constant mantra with SEAL officers. You can never lie to the guys— you can never make up or exaggerate a mission to get their blood going. Do that once and your credibility is shot.

If you can't obtain the real thing, find other ways to keep their blood flowing. SEALs may bitch and moan with a smile, but they'll actually enjoy it if you have them conduct one more building assault. They'll sit and fight with their buddies during a long ocean transit in a small boat, but afterward, when they talk about how lousy the weather was, or how Dawg almost froze to death, they'll have big smiles on their faces. Keep them pumped up like that and you can lead them anywhere.

THE TAKE-AWAY

Why are your people working for you? Are they looking for a safe haven or an opportunity? Whatever the reason is, it's probably not just about money. If it is, that 5 percent raise you've got waiting for them probably won't do the trick.

One thing you rarely hear from human resources consultants is that employees aren't paid enough. Yes, people are underpaid at times, and yes, people always want more money. But when people aren't being paid what they think they're worth—i.e., if it really is about the money—then they usually aren't around long enough to be counted.

So realize this: The leading motivator for employees isn't cash. It's job satisfaction. It's feeling appreciated for their input and work. It's having their opinions count. It's having the opportunity to meet a challenge head on with the resources they need.

In a study that's been repeated too often to discount (see the table below), managers felt that wages and job security were the most important factors in an employee's satisfaction, while employees felt that a full appreciation of their work and feeling "in" on things were the most important factors.

FACTORS	MANAGERS	EMPLOYEES
Full appreciation for work done	8	1
Feeling "in" on things	10	2
Help on personal problems	9	3
Job security	2	4
Good wages	1	5
Interesting work	5	6
Promotion/growth/opportunities	3	7
Personal loyalty to workers	6	8
Tactful disciplining	7	10

SOURCES:
Foreman Facts, Labor Relations Institute of NY (1946); Lawrence Lindahl, Personnel Magazine (1949). **Repeated with similar results by:** Ken Kovach (1980); Valerie Wilson, Achievers International (1988); Bob Nelson, Blanchard Training & Development (1991); Sheryl & Don Grimme, GHR Training Solutions (1997–2001).

SEALs are not loyal because of wages—there is little of that in the life of a SEAL. They are loyal because they believe in what they are doing, they believe in the impact they can have on the outcome of a mission, and they believe that they make a difference.

It's no different for employees in a large corporation or a small company. What's important at the end of the day is that they are recognized for their work. There are countless ways to accomplish this—even the smallest gesture of appreciation will go a long way. The alternative is to ignore the good work your people do, and that approach will go a long way as well, although you may not like the direction in which it takes you.

LESSON 9
IF YOU CAN'T GIVE THEM FRESH MEAT, GIVE THEM REMINDERS OF WHAT FRESH MEAT TASTES LIKE

THE MISSION

The SEAL organization is filled with stories, traditions, and rituals that help the SEALs maintain a positive outlook between operations. These are what keep the guys going when they can't go parachuting, shooting, or swimming. They're what keep the guys loyal to the program during those weeks when maintenance and paperwork have to be conducted. They're things like being thrown in the dip tank after a good job or having to buy a case of beer for the gang after your first parachute jump into the ocean. They provide a continual reaffirmation of the warrior culture to which the guys belong. They provide a continual reminder of operations that were conducted in the past and are currently being conducted.

The following story is one of the things that kept me alive. It's a story that was passed down to me by a chief, and it's about what Mike Thornton did in a war a couple of decades ago. Every commando knows this story. I'm sure there's a better description, but this is mine.

Thornton and a guy named Norris—who had already won the Congressional Medal of Honor for something else but didn't know it yet—went onto a beach together. They went in to call for fire, that is, to direct the naval gunfire of warships waiting offshore. There were just the two of them and their Vietnamese counterparts. They had done this kind of thing before.

When they got ashore, they climbed over a couple of sand dunes. After mounting one of the dunes, they saw someone with a gun, and he fired at them. So they shot him. Then a few more bad guys appeared from over the next dune, and they ducked down and shot them, too. Then more and more of the bad guys came over. Then still more of them. There were too many of them. Thornton and Norris began leapfrogging backward, taking turns firing while the other one ran. More and more of the enemy came streaming over the dunes. Was this the entire enemy army?

Thornton and Norris couldn't back up fast enough. They called for the warships to bomb the hell out of the place, even the spot where they were crouched. They were shooting the enemy left and right. Then Norris took some rounds, including one in his skull, and he went down. Thornton got over to him, all the time still killing more of the enemy, and Norris said, "Hey, little buddy" when he recognized Thornton. Then Thornton got Norris onto his back. And he got up. He took several rounds himself. At this point, he was fighting hand to hand with the enemy while at the same time carrying Norris. He somehow got to the water, shot up and bleeding everywhere, and he started swimming away. He was shooting and swimming, and dragging Norris with him. And they both lived.

That's what commandos do. If that doesn't impress you, you're already dead. It's the same with the account given to us about the SEAL one-star admiral who had bad luck on the mountainside one afternoon. It was icy cold, skin-freezing weather. They were most of the way up. Suddenly, the admiral got a finger jammed in a crack in the rock. The rock was sharp around his finger. When he couldn't keep a grip with his other frozen hand, he slipped, and the section of his finger that was trapped in the rock was ripped away from the rest of his hand. He wrapped a cloth around the cold, bloody stump. His climbing buddy rushed closer and yelled out if he was okay. "Yeah, but it's not like we're not going to finish this climb," the one-star said.

These are our leaders.

And if that's not enough, every team has its occasional Rattle Battle, where everyone gets geared up and takes a turn tearing through an obstacle course/shooting range from hell. Or it's Friday Monster-Mash, a run–swim–run–swim–carry the timber–run–pull-ups–swim–paddle across the bay event (or some other variation) in case someone needs to get cocky again. These events last for several hours. I put one on that began with a straight 2 minutes of push-ups, then continued with a cross-country run, for a mile of which you had to carry a telephone pole on your back. Everybody complained that I had put on an easy event. One boss in Panama liked to combine shooting, running, ladder climbing, swimming, and pull-ups, while carrying your full war load on your back.

What's behind this? Well, there's not always enough action to keep everyone busy. And during the downtime, you need something to keep the blood pumping and the men going.

THE TAKE-AWAY

Why are people working for you? Why are they staying on board and doing the drudge work in between exciting projects? What keeps them busy and interested when the going gets tough?

You need to create ways to remind people why they are working for you. And these had better be more than just an annual salary review. People are working for you because they like what they have, because they like the challenge. They enjoy the chase. And if they don't get that from you, they're going to look elsewhere for it.

Take our advice. Create some challenges. Create a culture of work and opportunity. Keep what you're doing alive by telling the stories of those who went before you. Use stories of your company's past accomplishments to illustrate the culture you want to maintain. Talk about other great companies to illustrate where you want to go.

If you don't keep them excited during down times, then it's just going to be another long day at the office for them.

LESSON 10
PROVIDE THOSE OTHER THINGS SO THAT THEY CAN FOCUS ON THEIR JOBS

THE MISSION

I knew a guy who was stationed overseas with his family at a location that didn't have a strong medical support system. Basically, they were living out in the bush. The electricity went out occasionally. The road to their location would wash away during the rainy season. Mosquitoes carrying dengue fever swarmed the area. A jaguar came and drank from a stream that ran through their neighbor's land.

The SEAL unit in the area was great. They gave the guy a radio for his wife, so that she could keep in contact with the other SEALs when the phones when out. And the command masterchief would occasionally drive out to check on things. But those things didn't make up for the inconsistent medical support. There was one time when his 2-year-old daughter got sick just as he was being deployed farther down range on an operation. So guess what was on his mind the entire time he was away.

Did he do his job? Yes. Did he have second thoughts about why he was doing it when he returned? He'd be a fool not to.

THE TAKE-AWAY

You don't have to study Maslow's hierarchy to understand the minimum requirements that people need if they are to keep going. You don't need to have a Ph.D. in human relations. You simply have to recognize that basic necessities have to be in place if people are going to concentrate on achieving superior goals.

Here are those basic necessities. They're pretty simple.

Pay

Ensure that they have enough.

Don't indulge people, unless that's the point of coming to work. If a guy wanted to be a millionaire, he'd be working for someone else. As long as a SEAL doesn't have to worry about his family back home, can afford an occasional night out at the cantina, and doesn't think he's being forgotten by the taxpayers, he's good to go in the field. If he doesn't get these things, he won't be thinking about the target in front of him.

Pay your employees a fair rate for their work (and we mean *fair*) and then forget all about the money. If it's really not enough, they'll let you know. Instead, focus on the rest of the equation. The more you bring up money, the more your employees will be reminded of it. Truly—it's not the most important thing.

Titles

Ensure that the title corresponds to the amount of respect the employee needs in order to do the job.

Titles must have meaning or they're just a stupid source of embarrassment. Honorary titles take away from real titles that do mean something. Honorary SEAL? What the hell is that? Honorary titles breed contempt. Don't give them out.

Give people with real titles the respect that they've earned. A SEAL goes through a lot to become a chief. He's collected lots of war stories. He's mastered lots of skills. He deserves to be treated differently. He deserves to be called "chief," not "you" or "hey, there." Part of his ability to make your platoon function depends on the rest of the platoon knowing that you treat him differently.

Admittedly, outside the military, titles often mean different things in different companies. You probably don't have the luxury of having a universal structure with well-defined titles like lieutenant, captain, and ensign. But it's pretty safe to assume that if you give someone a title akin to that of manager, then that person should have the freedom to manage her or his own time and actions. If you give someone a director's title, that person should have some approval control over his or her own budgets. Vice president, senior vice president, executive vice president, general manager—all these titles mean that the person has the experience to run the group or division. And if it's a C-level title—CEO, CFO, COO, CTO—then this means that the person holds sway.

Respect

You earn respect by giving it. Let people know when you think highly of them, and don't even think of bullshitting them.

SEAL team skippers respect the yeoman in the Admin Department, who sets SEALs' pay records, as much as they do those SEALs operating in the field. Sometimes more so. Why? Because he makes sure that everyone gets their checks. Whether or not sailors get respect has nothing to do with their job description. They get it for doing their jobs well.

But there's a difference between respecting a worker and sucking up to or coddling him or her. The skipper of a SEAL team respects his SEALs' ability to handle harsh criticism, to work late when required, and to accomplish tough goals without his having to hold their hands. You should do the same for your employees. Respect isn't based on hugging employees all the time or holding their hands—in fact, that's an insult because you aren't treating them as equals.

So how should you show respect? By treating everyone the same way. Offer everyone the same courtesies you enjoy receiving. Listen to their opinions. Give them the same honest feedback you want them to give you. But remember, respect doesn't mean giving people preferred status or breaking down your company's hierarchy for them. Respect doesn't mean coddling. Respect means treating them as responsible adults and expecting them to deliver on what they promise.

Recognition

Ensure that people know that you know how they're doing—both when they do well and when they do poorly.

It's hard to continuously put out great work if no one notices or cares. When SEALs have done good work, SEAL team leaders constantly remind their people that they know they've done good work. But they don't pass out accolades unless something's really been done.

For great accomplishments, the entire team forms in ranks and comes to attention. Platoon commanders write letters to their bosses, praising and recommending their team members. Chiefs slap their guys on the backs and tell the platoon commander to say something in front of the platoon about a deserving young team member.

The bad things get recognized too. It's equally important to recognize when things don't go well. After a horrible early ship-attack training session during which we took too long to secure the target and left one of our men on a deck without a back-up, I put out a severe, postmission message: *"That sucked, guys. This is the varsity, not the JV. We can do better than that. If you don't think you can, don't show up in the morning."*

If you're not getting the hint here, what we're talking about is treating people like adults. And that means praising the good and raising hell about the bad. Like respect, recognition doesn't just mean providing compliments when things go well. It means recognizing when things go wrong and acting accordingly.

Loads

Let everyone know that you'll protect the good performers from the poor performers.

A SEAL can't concentrate on static-line parachuting into a target if he thinks the guy who packed his parachute is a dirtbag. He can't focus on flying mini-subs long distances if he knows that the guy who charged the sub's batteries didn't know what he was doing. He can't focus on the apartment door in front of him if he knows the guy covering his back is suffering from a severe hangover.

The SEAL organization maintains several safeguards that protect SEALs from such fears. They're called performance standards. If you don't perform, you're out.

The process for becoming a SEAL platoon commander is strictly enforced. High standards are fiercely maintained. No exceptions. That means don't even think about fudging one of your guys' shooting qualifications, no matter how good friends you are. That also means losing the people who don't cut it.

If you can't do that in the workplace, then you're telling everyone that it's okay for profits to miss their mark, it's okay for somebody to not complete a job, and its okay to miss a project's completion date. It's okay because everyone is going to work at the level of the worst employee. And that is *not* okay.

If you don't hold the line, then everyone is going to suffer because you don't have the courage to enforce your own standards. How well do you think the good ones will focus on their jobs if they know that?

Trust

Ensure that they know you will be there for them.

My squad once rode a rubber boat far out from shore to meet a large submarine. An unexpected storm rolled in along the way. Large waves tossed our boat around. We needed more gas to beat back the wind and rain. Communications were down. Two of my guys, SEALs, were puking over the side. We couldn't see beyond the crest of the waves a few feet in front of us. At our rendezvous point, we were over the horizon, using up more gas to try to stay in place.

Assuming that we got to the right place, how did we know that the submarine would pick us up? After all, these weren't the kind of conditions in which subs like to surface and open their hatches. We knew because the sub was full of Navy people who, although we had never met, had passed through many of the same physical and emotional gauntlets we had overcome. They too had gotten their heads shaved when they had first come in. They too had dealt with screaming chiefs and impossible exams in training school. And, of course, my boss was on board the submarine, and we knew he would make that sub surface if he had to blow the ballast tanks all by himself.

That the submarine might not pick us up never entered out minds.

LESSON 11
IF SHARKS STOP SWIMMING FORWARD, THEY STOP BEING SHARKS

THE MISSION

When I was in Bangkok, I met a young SEAL officer who was just out of BUD/S. He was professional, ambitious, and hard working. He had been sent to us as the special operations liaison to the U.S. embassy in another country in Southeast Asia, and he was now supporting a political contingent from that country that was visiting Thailand. I was surprised to learn that we had such a liaison billet in that country. I also remarked that it was a great opportunity for someone so junior to be given such a position.

He explained that we didn't normally have such a billet to fill. However, there was a temporary glut of young SEAL officers at his particular SEAL team, and his commanding officer was determined to find ways to keep his junior officers busy. Rather then have them sit around watching other commandos keeping busy, his skipper had created new jobs that amounted to on-the-job training. Other excess junior officers were sent to special operations commands in Europe or the Middle East. Nothing would be worse than pumping a high-energy guy through the fires of BUD/S, jump school, dive school, and advanced training, only to have him sit and edit after-action reports at headquarters.

I had witnessed the slow destruction of a platoon in another location that had fallen prey to much of what the junior officer's skipper was trying to avoid. This platoon didn't have a clear mission. The commander of the joint operation of which the platoon was part had made it clear that he did not intend to use it. Meanwhile, there were limited training areas in the vicinity. The platoon members had nothing to do. Most of them ended up quitting within a year. They hadn't invested years of sweat and blood to sit on their asses. They could sell soap and make more money.

THE TAKE-AWAY

Resource allocation is part of being a leader. If you can't find any work for your team to do, then why have them around? As a team leader, you should always have a list of projects—projects that develop new business, projects aimed at process improvement, or projects aimed at strategic development, projects that force your people to rest. If you run out of projects, ask your team what needs to be done.

If you're running your team well, there should always be something to do. If there isn't, then it's time to disband. If you don't give your team anything to do, then people who are worth their weight are going to find something to do. And that includes looking for another job, freelancing for someone else, working on a hobby, or just enjoying the time off. Whatever it is they do, we can guarantee you, it's not going to be adding to your bottom line.

LESSON 12

LET IT BE KNOWN THAT YOU'LL GET RID OF PEOPLE WHO JUST SHOULDN'T BE PART OF THE TEAM—EVEN THE NICE PEOPLE

THE MISSION

Some of the best people in the world make the mistake of deciding that they should be SEALs. In my BUD/S class, there were lots of broken bones, a few cases of pneumonia and hypothermia, and several guys who just couldn't master diving physics. But there were also guys who were just plain in the wrong line of work.

This is what happens to those people. During their instruction, they indicate some weakness or hesitancy. The instructors identify the specific problem and pile it on. You're afraid of sharks? Fine; let's go for a midnight swim out in deep dark water after listening to several stories about shark attacks. If they like the guy, the rest of the class will encourage him, but eventually he'll be out there with his buddy, alone. Then he'll do it again the next night. And the next night.

Eventually, the person realizes that the drill of swimming where there might be sharks isn't going to go away. He runs to the bell in the corner of the compound and rings it three times. That means he's quit. Everyone in the compound, the instructors and the other students, can hear it. There's no question about what has happened.

When someone quits, he is brought inside. They counsel him about what a talented guy he is and how not making it through BUD/S doesn't reflect poorly on him. They try to determine how else he might be able to serve the Navy. They try to arrange for him to go on to flight school, or Explosive Ordnance Demolition school, or surface warfare school. They don't try to change his mind about quitting, though. That's a done deal.

In the meantime, the rest of the class hasn't stopped. They all know the guy has quit. Many of them know that he should have quit a long time ago. None of them think any less of him. He just wasn't cut out to be a SEAL. Soon he's forgotten completely. The ones that remain all feel a little more elite.

THE TAKE-AWAY

Of course, this is true in the business world as well. Jeff had a guy working for him years ago. He was a nice enough guy. He was always walking around and talking with everyone. He always had his headphones on, listening to music while he worked. Nobody really minded any of this, but it didn't take long to notice that his projects never seemed to progress to completion. His deadlines somehow got pushed back; his deliverables somehow were reduced. And when it came time to complete some major portion of his projects, it was always a nightmare.

The problem wasn't a lack of intelligence or skill; he simply didn't really want to work that hard. This was something Jeff could understand, but it meant that everyone else had to jump in and help out at the last minute.

When Jeff sat him down to discuss the problem, his response was that he was more of a big-picture person. The best way he could help the team, he said, was through his ability to strategize and come up with ideas. Hey, no problem. Jeff could understand that. He loves nothing more than sitting back and thinking up ideas for everyone else to implement. The problem was, there weren't and still aren't too many positions like that in the job market. And that certainly wasn't what he had hired him for. He had hired him to complete projects on time and on budget. To turn ideas into revenues by getting his hands dirty. Everyone else on the team did, and they usually had time left over to come up with some pretty damned good ideas as well.

Since he was a smart guy, Jeff gave him additional projects and worked through them with him, but he would invariably do everything at about 60 percent and leave the rest for someone else to pick up. Even after he was warned of what was pending, he continued to hand in incomplete proposals and projects, maintaining that this kind of work wasn't his strong suit.

In the end Jeff had to spend the time to document the problems and go through the human resources process of letting him go. During his exit interview, he was shocked that Jeff was letting a guy as brilliant as he was go. After all, he was an A student. He had an MBA. He came up with some great ideas. To him, the problem wasn't his abilities, it was everyone's inability to see how smart he was.

No argument, he was a bright guy. He just didn't want to do the job he had. He wanted to sit back and think. Thinking is great, but unfortunately somebody has to turn that thinking into revenue. Because without that, there is no company and there is no position to fill. And that was something he wasn't able to do.

We hope his new boss is able to let him sit back and think.

LESSON 13
SAVE THEM IF YOU CAN,
BUT RECOGNIZE WHEN YOU CAN'T

THE MISSION

In one of the teams I worked with, there was a fabulous operator who couldn't control his anger. The guy knew everything in his trade. He'd be the first to go through the door for you. But then he'd drink, and he was an angry, lousy drunk. And many of the people who saw him when he was drunk made the decisions about whether or not we'd be employed.

In the end, no matter how good someone is, behavior like that can cost the team its mission. And if it does, all the other team members will hate him, and they'll hate you as the leader for letting him do that to the team.

Fortunately, the chief was onto this guy. After the guy went too far one night, the chief grabbed him and got him back to base. We restricted him from going to town. We counseled him. We discussed the possibility of his getting professional help. We acknowledged that he was a great operator, but we told him honestly that he was screwing up the team. A long silence followed.

Cut forward several years. He's still on the team. He's still a great operator. He doesn't have any liabilities.

In another instance, I had a brilliant guy in my BUD/S class. He was super smart. He was strong. But he just couldn't seem to develop the skills necessary to lead men in physically awful and emotionally draining situations. He freaked out once and led a charge into simulated machine-gun fire. The instructors decided to give him an opportunity to learn, and to prove that they were wrong about him. For the next month, the amount of physical and emotional abuse he endured was phenomenal, but he didn't get much better at what he was supposed to do. As a classmate said, "He's like a dog who just won't go home."

He finally quit.

It rarely happens, but occasionally someone makes it all the way through BUD/S before his weakness surfaces. Once, a sharp former JAG made it all the way through BUD/S and got to a SEAL team before anyone realized that he actually had no sincere regard for his men. He didn't realize that there is no tenure within the SEAL organization. There is no statute of limitations. The SEAL team skipper threw him out. "But I'm a good SEAL," the guy said. "No," the skipper answered. "You're a good lawyer."

THE TAKE-AWAY

There is no reason to retain a bad employee or someone who doesn't want to be there. Try to improve such an employee. Attempt to get the employee to understand her or his importance to the team and how her or his actions affect the rest of the mission. But if the person doesn't change, then get rid of her or him. Don't play Florence Nightingale by continuously trying to improve an employee who just won't play ball.

To determine what to do, assess why an employee isn't working out. Identify the employee's weaknesses and determine a course of action based on the problem. Whether you have to fire someone, spend additional time training the person, add to the existing resources, or deal with motivational issues should be determined by the problems at hand.

The figure below may help in determining what to do with a problem employee. Based on the employee's motivation and skill level, identify what the actual issue is.

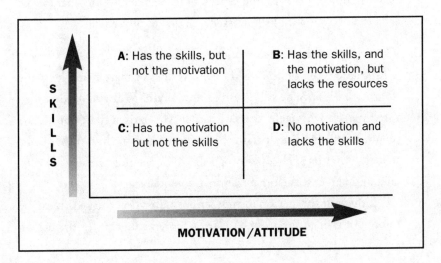

A: *The employee has the skills, but lacks the motivation to do the job.* Many stellar athletes attend BUD/S. That doesn't mean that they all put out. Sometimes they try to take it easy and hide in the middle of the pack, while the real stud is the guy whose heart is pounding as he tries to hang on to the rear. If the person has the skills but is not motivated to work, deal with him or her intensively. Identify why that person does or does not want to be a part of the team. If the employee is unmotivated because of salary or lack of opportunities, determine if you have the resources to change that. If the lack of motivation is due to a lack of opportunities, determine if the person has outgrown the position. Try to find a way to make this potential Ferrari run, but if it just won't, remove the person from the position; the person's frustration will only undermine the rest of the team.

B: *The employee has the skills and motivation, but lacks the resources to do the job.* Imagine ordering a hard-charging, experienced SEAL to take down a target with a lousy plan and the wrong weapons. It's happened. People die. You're screwing the guy over!

This is not a problem the employee can help you with. If you don't have the resources necessary to complete a project or the leadership to direct the resources, then you either have to reallocate the necessary resources or revise the expectations people have of what can be achieved. This is a leadership issue, not an employee issue.

C: *The employee has the motivation, but lacks the skills to do the job.* This is a new guy on the SEAL team. It doesn't matter that he made it through BUD/S; he still doesn't know anything. If you have a motivated person who lacks the skills, then you have a diamond in the rough. Even if you can't train that person or enable him or her to be trained, don't let such a person go. If you screw this one up, it's your fault and you cost the organization a potential star.

Either put this person in another position where the person can be tutored or trained for growth, or set achievement goals for the person to meet. Salaries may have to be revised to be appropriate to the person's skill level, but such a person should be retained. Where's there is an opportunity and a potential, use it to the limit of the potential.

D: *The employee has neither the skills nor the motivation to do the job.* Fire such people. They're loads. They'll pull others down. Don't waste your time trying to train, grow, or reposition them. Do yourself a favor and save everyone the time and trouble.

CHAPTER 6

NOW MAINTAIN YOUR MOMENTUM

LESSON 1
IF YOU NEED TO SCREAM,
YOU NEED TO PRACTICE

THE MISSION

During basic demolition training, SEAL students set their explosives on their targets, lay out their electric firing wires to the bunker, and sit behind a huge wall of dirt and concrete. One of them yells "Fire in the hole," squeezes a pulse generator, and detonates all the charges simultaneously. A huge, dull sound rolls through the chamber. Everyone presses their hands against their ears. The ground shudders. A shower of fresh dirt patters like rain against the bunker roof.

If it's the first time students are on the demolition range, they'll want to shout out their approval, but they'll have to refrain. Everyone has to listen quietly for additional explosions resulting from charges that might not have been constructed correctly. That is the complete opposite requirement that the student who fired the shot was tasked with. He had to yell "Fire in the hole" as loud as he could so that the whole universe could hear him. Not doing so wouldn't have gone down well with the instructors, who would have wanted him to shake the roof with his voice. By screaming out loud, he'd warn everyone in the area that an explosive was about to go off.

Neither act—sitting silently after a brilliant accomplishment or screaming at full bore in front your buddies—is natural. Sitting, by itself, is easy. But it's hard to sit quietly when your heart is pumping through the roof and your neurons are firing overtime. Screaming is easy, too. But get someone who's never screamed before in front of a room of people, and sometimes it's a disappointment. Sometimes you get a three-quarter yell resonating with embarrassment and self-consciousness. This happens even when people yell that a speeding train is about to derail, the building is about to collapse, or someone's just fallen overboard. *But people will stare at me if I scream.* Read about screaming all you like, but until you're red in the face from doing it, you won't know how you'll react or what you'll sound like. And if you're too self-conscious about what strangers might think—if you're too shy to accomplish the simple task of screaming—how likely are you to act boldly during the far more difficult leadership tasks that lie ahead? That's what irks the SEAL instructors.

Get the reason for the drill?

SEALs solve this through practice. BUD/S students scream out that there's an ambush. They scream out full muster in the morning before getting wet and sandy. They scream out that missiles are inbound. They scream out for everyone to get their weapons on line at once during a firefight. Not hysterically, but so everyone can hear above the ear-pounding roar of gunfire.

This is called practical application. And practical application continues throughout SEAL training. Why? Because getting your feet wet is the best way to learn how to swim. You've learned from your manual how to tie a half hitch? Great, now get in the water, swim the length of the pool underwater, and tie a half hitch for us. And then a square knot. Classroom training in dive physics is soon followed by construction of a depth profile that you'll swim that night. Medical instruction is followed by sticking an IV needle in your teammate's vein to practice giving him plasma. A class on shooting tactics is followed by long hours on the range. Instructor so-and-so can talk circles about how to construct a shape charge out of plastic explosive. But it's not until you actually begin cutting C-4 and measuring detonation cord that you really learn how to blow a hole in the side of a tank's armor plating and know exactly what it will do on the other side.

SEALs teach leadership the same way. By forcing students to get in and get their hands dirty. The key to success—the only key—is to put leadership theory into practice.

In the beginning of BUD/S, we were being mauled pretty badly on a daily basis, which is pretty much the plan. One afternoon, when we managed to gather behind some buildings for 5 minutes to figure how to face the madness, one of the other officers laid it out for the rest of us. "This is a great opportunity," he said. Everyone looked at him. *Are you crazy?* "You should be using every chance you have to try out new leadership skills," he continued. "You're not going to have this opportunity for long." He was right. No matter what we did in the short term, pain, failure, and punishment were going to follow. We were all going to be naked and cold. The point was to learn while we were suffering in the short term so that we would suffer less in the long term.

His message?

Get over your self-consciousness. Get out there and practice screaming, and guiding, and moderating, and leading. It's the only way you'll succeed.

THE TAKE-AWAY

So here's where the rubber hits the road. You have a choice. You can say, "I'm done," put the book on a shelf, and never do a thing. Or you can take action. If you do the former, don't expect anything to get better. If you do the latter, then at least you have a fighting chance.

So, go into your office, speak to a subordinate, peer, or boss, and try out a new technique. Don't get hung up trying to plan out the conversation word for word. Make a few notes about what you want to achieve and how you plan to get there. Consider his or her possible reactions. Plan how you'll react in return. Then do it. Bring someone back in line.

Demonstrate that you're on board. Communicate a new way to go. It won't go as smoothly as you like at first. You are going to screw up sometimes. But don't worry—that's life. In the end, you'll come away proud of yourself and change will have happened.

When Jon quit a job in corporate banking to join the SEALs, he was entering new territory. But he jumped in, he made mistakes, he learned lessons the hard way—by doing it. When Jeff quit his job at a public relations firm to enter the film industry, he had no idea where it would lead. But he jumped in, made mistakes, learned lessons the hard way, and grew. Yes, both paths were tough. But it was a hell of a lot more productive and rewarding than forever reading books about the SEALs or the film industry and never giving it a chance.

Your situation is no different. This book—every book on leadership and teamwork–is useless unless you put some of what you've read into practice. Will you make mistakes? Of course. SEAL students practicing sliding IV needles into one another's forearms for the first time is a guarantee that there will be lots of bruised arms the next day. But don't be afraid. You will get better, faster than you think. You will shoot more accurately, save more lives, communicate more effectively, command more loyalty, produce better products, and go to sleep more often knowing that you made a big difference.

Scared? You should be. But that's just your body's way of saying it's alive.

Now go to work.

INDEX

Access, limiting, 77–80
Accountability, 59–62
  and leadership, 118
  personal, 65
Adaptation, 105
Afghanistan, xiii, 21–23
Africa, 32
Anger, 134–135
Anticipation:
  of chaos, 25
  of problems, 20, 103–105
  of technological advancement, 25
  of the unforeseen, 26
Authority, 72, 117–118

Bangkok, 210
Bank Manager, The, 113–114
Basic needs, 205–209
Basic Underwater Demotion School
  (BUD/S), x–xi, 41, 43
Benchmarks (for success), 33, 53–54
Big picture, 74, 99–101
Boats, coastal patrol, 29–30
Bosnia, xiii, 32
Boundaries, building, 80–81
Bruckheimer, Jerry, 112
BUD/S (see Basic Underwater Demotion
  School)

Cambodia, 199
Cannibalization, 81
Capabilities, maintaining, 41–42
Chain of command, 60
  enforcement of, 128–131
  exceptions to, 79–80
  and limiting access to yourself as leader,
  77–80
  respecting your own, 78
Change, 105
Chaos, leadership and, 103–105
Chile, 186
Chrysler, 17
Civilians, 22
CNN, 19
Coastal patrol boats, 29–30
Colombia, 186
Command master chiefs, 44
Commanding officers, 44
Communication:
  and chain of command, 129
  lines of, 75–76
  without retribution, 65

  of trust, 141–143
  two-way, 74
Congress, 29
Contingency planning, 14
Coronado Bridge (San Diego, CA), 142
Country Club Manager, The, 113
"Cowboy," 115–116
Culture, 43
  and downtime, 202–205

Daimler-Benz, 17
Decision-making:
  need for, 93–98
  and pyramid organizational structure,
  69–70
  and timing, 89–91
  and tough decisions, 106–108
Direction, providing, 101–103
Discipline, unnecessary, 144–146
Downtime, 202–205

Eastern Europe, 18, 46–47, 131
Ecuador, 36, 96
Email, 76, 131
Employees, 126–128; 131–132, 136–138
  key, 197–199
  as recruiters, 194–195
  retention of best, 188–191
Enron, 138
Established procedures, 44
Executive officers (XOs), 44

Firing (of employees), 126–128
Flat land organizational structure, 70–71
Flexibility, 26, 68, 105
Ford Motor Company, 175
Forecasting problems, 26

Gates, Bill, 112
Germany, 36
Goals, 10–54, 63–65
Grenada, xiii
Gulf of Oman, 24
Gulf War, 11–12, 196

"Hanoi Hilton," 31
Harassment, 79
Hierarchy, 68
Hierarchy of needs, 205
High standards, setting, 186–188, 208–209
"Hockey stick profits," 13

Incompetence, 79
Indispensability, myth of, 108–110
Individual contributions, evaluation of, 65
Infighting, 81
Inspirational leadership, 121–122
Intelligence officers, 46
Iran hostage crisis, 36, 105

Jacks-of-all-trades, 38
Job satisfaction, 201

Kennedy, John F., x
Khmer Rouge, 200
Knowledge leadership, 120–121

"La Pilota," 133
Labor supply, 4
Latvia, 186
Layoffs, 3
Leadership, xi, 4, 84–146
Leanness, 3
Lines of communications, 75–76
Loads, 208–209
"Lone Ranger," 115
Long-term goals, 43–45
Los Angeles Times, 16
Loyalty, xi, 197, 202

The Manager Who Can't Be Satisfied, 114–115
Managers:
   ensuring success of, 159–161
   fighting with, 162–164
Maslow, Abraham, 205
Meetings, 82–83
Mentors, 154–155
Micromanagement, 140
Microsoft, 26, 112
Middle East, 24, 134–136, 181
Mission(s):
   avoiding manufactured, 29–30
   backward planning for, 39–46
   defining success of, 31–33
   establishing objectives for, 33
   evaluating success of, 33
   and leadership, 87–88
   planning team around, 37–39
   risk assessment for, 34–37
   team and success of, 64
Mob mentality, 58, 61–62
Mobility, 26
Money, 201
Moral leadership, 122–123
Motivation, 200–202
Movement Over Urban Terrain (MOUT), 93, 95

Mussolini, Benito, 36

Navigation systems, 21
Navy, 29
Needs, basic, 205–209
Niche specialties, 38
Normandy, xii
Norris (Vietnam War combatant), 203

Objectives (see Goals)
O'Grady, Scott, 32
Okinawa, xii
Olympic games (Munich, 1972), 36
Operations officers, 45
Opinions, voicing, 162–164
Organizational integrity, xi
Organizational leadership, 120
Organizational structure, 55–83
Ownership (of actions), 176–178

Panama, xii
Pay, 206
Personal accountability, 65
Personality traits, 39
Peru, 36, 96, 186
Physical conditioning, xi
Planning, backward, 39–46
Planning (for meetings), 82
Platoon commanders, 46
Pol Pot, 199
Poland, 186
Prioritizing, 48–50
Problems, solutions and, 181–182
Procedures, established, 44
Productivity, 130
Project leaders, 73
Public relations, 193
Pyramid organizational structure, 69–70

Quality teams, 184–186

Realistic goals, 11–15
Recognition, 207–208
Recruiters, employees as, 194–195
Research and development, 30
Respect, 207
Responsibility, 117
Rewards:
   for maintaining chain of command, 78–79
   for real achievements, 196–197
Ringmasters, 57–59
Risk, 34–37, 136–138
Rituals, 178–180, 202–205
Rivalry, interservice, 18
Romania, 186

Rotating cycle organizational structure, 71–72

Screamers, 112–113
Senior management, 46–48
September 11, 2001 terrorist attacks, 21, 24, 76
Serbia, 18
Short-term goals, 45–46
Skills, 39
Smart bombs, 21–22
Solutions, 181–182
Somalia, xii, 18
Sony, 26
SOPs (Standard Operating Procedures), 174
Special Operations Command, 105
Standard Operating Procedures (SOPs), 174
Standards, setting high, 186–188, 208–209
Status meetings, 74
Structure, organizational (*see* Organizational structure)
Subordinates, limiting number of direct, 73
Swimming with Sharks (film), 175

Targets, 21–22
Team building, 183–217
Team(s), 41, 73–74, 147–182
Technical expertise, xi
Technical leadership, 119–120

Terrorists, 22
Thailand, 210
Thornton, Mike, 43, 202–204
Titles, 206–207
Traditions, 133–134
Training/training officers, 45–46, 79–80
Trickle-down effect, 159–161
Trust, 43, 209
    and chain of command, 78
    communicating, 141–143
    in subordinates, 79
Tyco, 138

United States, 36
USS. Stennis, 24, 136–137, 157

Values, implied, 178–180
Versatility, 26
Vietnam War, xii, 31, 43
"Volcano, the" (leader), 112–113

"Warning orders," 200
World War II, xii
Worldcom, 138

XOs (executive officers), 44

Yugoslavia, 18

ABOUT THE AUTHORS

JON CANNON graduated from Tulane University with a B.A. in History. He then joined the Navy. After graduating from Officers Candidacy School in Newport, Rhode Island, he was assigned to SEAL basic commando training, called Basic Underwater Demolition School (BUD/S), in San Diego. Jon Cannon was the only U.S. officer to graduate with his BUD/S class out of the 13 officers who tried.

During the following 10 years as a SEAL, Lt. Cmdr. Cannon traveled through the Far East, Latin America, Europe, the Mediterranean, the South Pacific, the Middle East, and Africa. He was involved in operations during the Cold War, the Gulf War, the Drug War, a war between Ecuador and Peru, Bosnia, and the opening of Eastern Europe before resigning his commission in 1998, shortly after being promoted to Lieutenant Commander.

In 2000, he received an MBA from the University of Michigan. He was called back to active duty following September 11. He spent the next 10 months forward-deployed overseas.

JEFF CANNON graduated from Syracuse University with a B.S. in Accounting and a B.S. in Business Law. He started his professional career with Burson Marsteller before moving to Los Angeles, where he started a small production group to develop and produce documentaries, commercials, and sponsored programming for numerous clients.

Returning to the world of advertising, Jeff worked with the Evans Group, a Los Angeles–based agency. He created and managed the interactive department for a Santa Monica–based design firm and headed up online marketing for *The Los Angeles Times*.

In 1998 Jeff wrote a leading online marketing book entitled *Make Your Website Work for You* for McGraw-Hill. After running a successful online agency for over two years, he joined DraftDigital as Senior Vice President of Interactive Marketing.